FINANCIAL FREEDOM FOR LAWYERS

How to build and manage your wealth as a legal professional

Jeremy Pooley

Rethink

First published in Great Britain in 2026
by Rethink Press (www.rethinkpress.com)

Contents

Introduction

Welcome to the first step towards financial freedom. Whether you have just started as a trainee solicitor or barrister, recently been promoted to partner in your firm or are an experienced KC starting to think about winding down, this book will provide you with helpful tips and detailed strategies to help you to achieve financial freedom, to create the future – away from the courtroom, chambers or office – that you want for you and your family.

Although this book has been written particularly for legal professionals, most of the content applies equally to individuals in different professions. If you are not from the legal profession, please do not think this book cannot be of assistance to you.

If you are self-employed, as many in the legal profession are, you are solely responsible for your own retirement planning. In addition, you have to ensure that you have adequate protection for any time you are unable to work, and, fundamentally, you need to protect your family financially in the event of your untimely death.

Making decisions in these areas can be difficult, with financial jargon often being unfamiliar and possible solutions complex and time-consuming to understand. The time and mental capacity pressure that a successful career in the legal profession entails can make it difficult for you to set aside time to consider your own long-term planning.

I have spent the past fifteen years working with individuals in the legal profession to help them to achieve their long-term goals. Those individuals range from former supreme court judges seeking help to be able to live a fulfilling life in retirement, while still helping their children and grandchildren; to legal text editors, whose demanding clients and failing eyesight meant that the final five years of their careers could be challenging, but where I could demonstrate that they could retire immediately.

I work with a significant number of partners at Magic Circle law firms, helping them to balance extremely demanding careers with planning for the future and ensuring that their families will be well provided for, whatever the future holds. This work also involves working with senior associates who are hoping to one day become a partner and need to put in place the building blocks of long-term planning, and working with a range of hugely successful lawyers, barristers and judges as they manage the transition from being at the top of their game professionally to enjoying a rewarding and stimulating life after they retire.

In the legal profession you are faced with complex and mentally taxing work, which often needs to be completed to tight deadlines and with complete accuracy. For many, team management responsibilities are added, without any allowance within the volume of billable work that must be achieved. This can make setting aside the time to consider your own financial decisions difficult, resulting for some in decisions being put off and financial planning being left on the back burner. Having no clear plan for your financial future can cause increased stress and anxiety. In the times when you do have a moment to think about your own finances, there can be a feeling of helplessness in not knowing what to do and not being able to set aside enough time to tackle these issues.

Understanding exactly how much is enough and having a clear strategy to achieve it will not only massively improve your changes of achieving financial freedom; it will also reduce stress around your own personal finances, allowing you to focus on family, friends and passions outside of work. This may even make you more productive within your work environment. From the experience I have built up, working with individuals with similar challenges, I am uniquely placed to be able to provide helpful guidance and support to ensure you are able to achieve the things that are most important to you and your family.

As couples make up the majority of family structures, I have referred to spouses and partners within the book, but the information is equally valid for single individuals. It can be even more relevant when divorce or separation impacts financial planning work that has already been carried out and requires a full rethink.

Within this book I will introduce you to all of the ingredients required to create a detailed and robust long-term financial plan. I will also cut through the financial jargon to let you know exactly what you require to be able to make smart financial decisions. By implementing these steps, you will be able to ensure you and your family have the secure financial future that your hard work and dedication have merited, whatever life throws at you.

I will lift the lid on the myths and secrets of the financial industry and provide you with the expertise, knowledge and guidance that many of your colleagues and friends pay significant sums for in investment management and advice fees.

I will introduce you to a five-stage process – my DREAM approach – which is designed to define what your future should look like and the steps required to make that happen. The five stages, covered in the five parts of this book, are:

1. **D**efine your vision: To be able to build a plan that allows you to achieve all the things that are important to you, we first need to understand what those things are. We'll look at planning the future over the short, medium and long term to understand what good progress looks like and to ensure you have a clear plan of where you want to get to.

2. **R**eview your current situation: We will look in more detail at what you have achieved so far, understanding the progress you have already made and whether you have all of the necessary building blocks for success in place or need to add more. As part of this process, we will consider your values and how they impact financial and life decisions.

3. **E**stablish your plan: This is the stage in which you will start to build your plan for achieving the things you outlined in Part One. We will look at all of the components that need to be included and consider how to document your plan so you have a clear roadmap of the steps you need to take.

4. **A**ct on it: Once the plan is built, we will look at the action you need to take to implement the plan and to ensure you get the required results. We will also consider some of the challenges and obstacles that could stand in your way or stop you from achieving your goals.

5. **M**onitor and modify: In this final stage we will look at the steps you need to take to keep your plan on track. We will also uncover the process to follow when your vision of the future changes, as it inevitably will over time.

By following this DREAM approach, everybody has the ability to create a great future for themselves. With hard work and the expertise provided within this book, there is no reason you cannot make a reality of those extraordinary things – a reality you only dare dream about. Throughout this book I will make reference to my own and my clients' personal experiences. These are not intended to give the impression that I have always made the right decisions – I certainly haven't – but to provide examples that will be helpful as you navigate similar situations.

The journey you will undertake as you consider your long-term financial future will need to be introspective. That includes an element of self-appraisal that none of us find easy, but it can be illuminating and powerful.

PART ONE
D – DEFINE YOUR VISION

With this process you will consider the things that are important to you in life and define what you would like to achieve, and you will prepare initial small steps and then the larger plans needed to realise your goals. We will consider what it would take for you to get to a point where you are happy with each aspect of your life, understanding that it is impossible to work on all at the same time. Your current demanding role likely means you won't be able to devote time and energy to all areas simultaneously.

We will then consider debt management, to understand the debt you have now and may have in the future, and how it can be efficiently managed.

It is important to spend enough time defining your vision, as without knowing where you would like to get to, it will be much harder for you to get there. In most cases this should be a joint exercise with your partner, if you have one; a shared vision of the future will help when difficult decisions need to be made. I have, however, come across plenty of people who have completed their financial planning entirely separately from their partner, which is an approach that clearly works.

1
Your Ideal Future

While we will go much deeper into what we want to achieve later in this first part of the book, at this stage it is helpful to have an idea of the things you would like to achieve during your lifetime. This will include short-term, medium-term and long-term ambitions. Those ambitions will carry different levels of significance and priority, with some being things you would like to be able to do in later life and others being fundamental to your happiness.

Where are you going?

The first question I tend to ask prospective clients is, *What prompted you to get in touch with me?* Using the same approach, I would like you first to think about what prompted you to pick up this book and start reading it.

Typically there is an initial trigger that gets people thinking about their financial future, and it is normally a problem that needs to be solved. This could be a pension contribution that needs to be made before a deadline or a distribution that needs to be invested. Often the trigger is an immediate requirement, in much the same way that many suddenly visit the dentist when they have toothache. Planning our financial future, though, is something we should do proactively, working with purpose to achieve the things that are important to us.

Normally I suggest working with your spouse or partner and having a bit of fun thinking about the future you would like to build, without the pressure at this stage of having to work out how you will do it.

The purpose of this exercise is to gain a high-level idea of where you want to get to as a couple and some of the destinations you would like to visit on the way. This is simply putting into words the thoughts you both have, some of which you will probably have talked about and some that you may not have yet discussed. At this stage try not to pass judgement on each other's suggestions. You are not committing yet to embark on that journey, so don't worry too much if your partner's destination appears to differ from your own. Keep it light and fun and try to flesh out what these things will be like in a little more detail.

We have now completed the first step. Together, you have opened the conversation about what the future will look like and started to build towards it.

As a reminder, you can of course complete this exercise alone if you do not have a spouse or partner.

George Kinder – the godfather of financial planning

George Kinder worked initially as a tax adviser in Cambridge, Massachusetts, before moving into financial advice and financial planning.

He felt in this work that too many advisers focused on the products and not on what the individuals want to achieve with their money. This led George to write a hugely influential book, *The Seven Stages of Money Maturity*, which looked at our early memories and experiences and how we can learn to have a better relationship with money.[1] It also resulted in him founding *life planning*, which is financial planning with a focus on individuals and the lives they would like to lead. It is a movement which has grown significantly in popularity over recent years, resulting in more financial

1 G Kinder, *The Seven Stages of Money Maturity: Understanding the spirit and value of money in your life* (Random House USA, 2000)

advisers seeking a better understanding of what is truly important to their clients and working with them to help them achieve their deeply held desires.

George has gone on to write many additional books, related to personal finance and other areas. He also teaches financial planners an approach to uncover the things that are truly important to their clients, through the use of three questions. The first is a high-level question, which tends to generate materialistic responses. The second question proposes a scenario and asks a question related to that scenario. The final question builds on the scenario in question two and probes that scenario further. Through these simple questions, individuals are required to think about the things that are most dear to them. Through this process, they are able to articulate their priorities in a manner they have possibly never even considered before and almost certainly have not shared with their partners or loved ones. This process can add meaning to the financial planning journey and increase the motivation to follow through with plans, particularly when they require sacrifices that are hard to make.

If you would like to know more, you could find a copy of *Life Planning for You,* which provides an easy-to-follow guide to George's work.[2]

2 G Kinder, *Life Planning for You: How to design and deliver the life of your dreams* (Serenity Point Press, 2014)

Vision for the next five years

As mentioned above, to make changes over the long term, we first need to look at the near future. All change starts with small adjustments, and to build a plan for change, we need first to review our current position.

Looking at how you feel now about a range of areas in your life is a good starting point, breaking those areas down into nine categories:

1. Family
2. Health
3. Hobbies and interests
4. Learning
5. Spirituality
6. Work
7. Home
8. Finances
9. Community

The first stage of defining your vision is to score yourself out of ten for where you are now. It may be that in some areas your score is low because it is of low importance, and that is fine.

Next, pick two or three areas in which you wish to make an improvement, as it may not be possible to work on all areas at the same time. First, record what a ten would look like. Try to do this in the first person, as if this has already happened and you are looking at what it feels like to be in this position. For example, if health is an area in which you want to improve, your analysis of what a ten looks like might be as follows:

> *I wake up at 6.30am, feeling refreshed. I prepare for my 7am yoga class with Sonia, something I look forward to each Tuesday and Thursday.*
>
> *By the time the class finishes at 8am, I feel strong and calm and ready to face the day.*
>
> *After a healthy breakfast of eggs and avocado, I get changed into my work clothes. I enjoy the feeling of being able to wear tailored shirts these days, since I hit my target weight two years ago. My weight has been consistent, meaning my new wardrobe fits me well at all times. During a busy day of back-to-back meetings as we work through a complex case, I make sure I take the time to have a salad for lunch from the new deli around the corner from the office.*
>
> *After work I head to the gym on the way home, for a swim and relaxation. I begin with fifty lengths of the pool to see if I can match my best time. I then spend twenty minutes unwinding in the jacuzzi, before heading home to make a healthy meal for the family. After some relaxation and downtime, it is time for stretches and bed. It's been a tough day!*

This may be a million miles away from what your life is like now, but if health is an area you want to improve, visualising an ideal situation will help you consider what steps you can take in the next five years to move towards that target. The key – for any area you want to improve – is to find little steps that can be achieved to help you move forwards, and that process of small incremental progression will lead you to where you want to be. This is more effective than trying to make sweeping changes to much of what you do, as often these changes last only a few weeks and end in failure and a loss of motivation.

Progress might be as simple as, *Twice a week I will walk to or from the station rather than getting a taxi or taking the car or public transport.*

I spent many years working on the fifth floor of an office block. When I started to focus on improving my health, I decided that instead of taking the lift to my office, I would take the stairs. For the first couple of months it was really hard work to motivate myself to do this. If I was tired or in a rush, I would think, *I'll get the lift today and get back on it tomorrow*, but I tried to resist that urge. If I did give in and took the lift, I ignored that I had failed and got my self-discipline back on track the following day. After a few months, all this had become a habit, and I automatically headed for the stairs. I was no longer out of breath when I got to the third floor, as I had initially been – I could now get to the fourth floor before my breathing changed. Sometimes, I would still think, *I'm tired; I'll get the lift today*, but I would find I had unthinkingly started to climb the stairs when I got to them. I wasn't until I reached the second floor that I would remember I had planned to take the lift, by which time there was no point.

This example illustrates that if you make a change to your lifestyle and do it consistently for a couple of months, you will form a new habit. Once you have done that, you no longer need motivation to continue to do it.

Let's think forward to when you have selected the areas you want to work on. You know what ten looks like (however unachievable that feels at the moment), and you have worked out the baby steps you need to take towards that. You now need to map out further baby steps that would take you to somewhere in five years – steps that will move the needle towards a ten in these areas. Keep reviewing them at six-month intervals, and don't try to do too much at once.

If there is a challenging target in one area, make things easier in another and try to alternate this between the different areas. Motivation is a finite resource, so be careful not to use it all in one area, as you will then find it hard to pursue other things you want to. This is particularly important because progressing your career in the legal world already requires a lot of your motivation.

It is also important to forgive yourself for the times when you omit intended actions towards your targets. Tomorrow is another day. If today took you away from the target, put it out of your mind and just aim for the target again tomorrow. Don't try to make up what has been lost, and don't dwell on the disappointment. We all have off days, and the odd day you don't meet your target won't prevent you from succeeding, whereas giving up certainly will.

Time pressure

For most of the corporate lawyers I work with, time is the scarcest commodity, and I am certain this is the case in other areas of law. Barristers, for example, are particularly strapped for time while in the middle of cases, although they sometimes have a gap before the next case, which can provide some respite (or anxiety about where the next big case will come from).

Not having enough time will impact on your ability to work on all areas of life. It may be that you have to wait, for example, to work on areas such as community work and hobbies. Provided you are sacrificing the areas that feel less important at this stage, though, that is fine, and it can be a necessary compromise.

In the same way, the amount of progress you make in each area may be slow. If you are working, though, towards a target you have identified in an area of your life you would like to improve, however small the target and however slow the progress, it is still better than doing nothing and probably better than the vast majority of other people.

Finances

Given that you are reading this book, I suspect a financial improvement is fairly high on your agenda, so let's look at that in a little more detail.

We have already covered how you might record what a ten looks like, but you are probably not expecting to get there within the next five years. You instead need to consider the smaller steps you can take to move towards your long-term target.

Depending on your starting point, the first small step might be, *Over the coming six months, I am going to become more aware of my spending and the cost of my lifestyle.* One step you might take to achieve that is to review your bank statement and credit card bill at the end of each month. This might involve you taking an hour a month to categorise your spending and get a better handle on what you spend money on. At this stage, unless you have a critical need to, you shouldn't make any attempt to adjust your spending or critique your purchases or spending. It is simply a case of understanding the cost of your lifestyle.

At the end of the six months, you will have a good idea of what you are spending and will be ready to see patterns. Are you saving as much as you would like? Are there things you are spending money on that provide you with little or no value? Are there high-value things you should spend more on?

After those six months, look for the next small step, which might be, *I'm going to save an additional 10% of each distribution*. If you struggle to spend money on yourself, the small step could be that you will treat yourself to something that feels extravagant from each distribution.

On the financial side of things, what does good look like? What would need to happen over the next five years for you to be happy with the progress you make? It might be that, by the end of the five years, you want to have added £50,000 to your pension and have reduced your outstanding mortgage by 25%, while still being able to enjoy the comfortable lifestyle you currently have. In the previous exercise you have discovered that you would be able to save an extra £5,000 from each distribution by simply being savvier with your day-to-day spending. This will help you to achieve your target, but it won't be enough on its own. You therefore need to look at what else you can do.

If a condition is that you maintain your current lifestyle, you can't make significant reductions to holidays or entertaining, so you need to look at other ways, for example:

- Making sure that your savings and investments are properly structured could help.
- Making small overpayments on the mortgage, when you can, will make a difference.
- If the firm has a good year and distributions are more than expected, rather than having a better holiday than planned, could you save most of that extra income?
- As you reduce your outstanding mortgage with lump sums, why not keep the repayments the same? This will additionally reduce the outstanding balance and pay off more capital, creating a snowball effect, as the interest payments will reduce further with each payment, meaning you continue paying off more capital. This option is less attractive, of course, if you are in the early years of a large mortgage and your mortgage payments are most of your monthly drawings!

It is in taking the small steps that you will achieve the big goals, rather than trying to make big sacrifices or doing without things you really enjoy or want. You work extremely hard, and none of us know the future, so you do need to live for today as well as saving for tomorrow. In my experience, those who try to make big sacrifices can do so for only so long before their willpower gives way. They then make extravagant purchases, often putting themselves further back in their planning than would have been the case if they had done nothing.

Monitoring

The only other thing you need to do throughout your five-year vision process is to set up some kind of monitoring. This is the opportunity to assess progress and to enjoy your success or refocus, and it should take place around every six months.

Monitoring may best be timed to happen just before a distribution or bonus payment or salary review. This could be particularly helpful because we all have a tendency to spend forthcoming additional income in our minds before it arrives. Reviewing your progress will let you know how much can be allocated to lifestyle and enjoyment now and how much needs to be focused on the future.

SARAH'S VISION

Sarah has been through transitions before; she is a world leader when it comes to change. After an early career as a bright and talented associate, she was made a partner at a much younger age than most of the associates she trained with. As a young partner, she was seen as the rising star of the firm and potentially one of their highest fee earners.

Sarah knew something wasn't right, though. Despite the success and acclaim from her colleagues and from peers at other firms, she wasn't feeling happy. For a number of years, she hid those feelings, from herself as much as from others. She tried to distract herself with expensive clothes and shoes as a reward for her work, which no longer fulfilled her.

In the end, Sarah's body made the decision that her mind was unable to. She suffered a serious health issue brought on by stress.

This forced Sarah to take time away from work and to reassess. It became clear to her, fairly quickly, that her career as a lawyer was over. In her early thirties, with no other skills (as she saw it) and a desire to maintain the comfortable lifestyle she had built, she was left wondering what she should do.

Sarah retrained as a business coach and built a successful coaching business. She worked, initially, with people in the legal profession, as she had a burning desire to help people going through the same thing she had experienced. Over time, the success of her work in this area resulted in coaching work across many different industries and businesses. She had been able to help a huge number of people build and develop their careers, and her drive and creativity allowed her to build a range of programmes and products. She now outsources much of her work to a talented team of coaches – people she has met on her journey, some of whom she mentored along the way.

Sarah reflects on her health scare as being a positive turning point in her life. It enabled her to move on from what she had spent her childhood and early career working towards (but not enjoying once she got there) to a career that was much more fulfilling. It allows her to use her talent and creativity in a way that helps others and is aligned to her values.

This experience taught Sarah how to manage transitions in her life and be able to quickly make adjustments when they are needed. Knowing what is important to her and ensuring she protects those things has become the heart of her approach.

Summary: Your ideal future

As you start to consider the future you would like to build, we have covered the following areas:

- Current satisfaction with different areas of life
- Small steps of improvement to make
- Setting a strategy for progress over a five-year period
- Monitoring progress and making adjustments when they are needed

By considering where you are now, where you most want to get to in the future and the first steps to get there, you have completed the vital first stage of your journey towards financial freedom.

2
Long-Term Planning

Now that you have clarity over what you will achieve over the next five years, let's think about the longer term.

What does great look like over ten years?

This is an important time frame. As any of us old enough to have passed more than one significant milestone knows, time passes very quickly. Ten years from now, however, much will have changed. If you currently have young children, for example, they will have gone from needing your help in every task, including playing with their toys, to spending all of their time in their rooms and speaking in words of only one syllable!

Your professional life

Just as you will experience changes in your personal life, a decade will mark significant differences in your career. Whether you are an associate now and hope to make partner soon or an experienced barrister hoping to make silk, or if you are coming towards the end of your legal career, ten years will likely lead to a significant transition of some description.

Within a decade, a number of things will happen to us over which we have little or no control. Some events will be great, others less so, and undoubtedly there will be some real challenges to work through. By completing thorough planning, you won't avoid the negative, and you will still have real struggles to get through. Being more deliberate in your focus, though, can help to ensure that you head in the direction you want to.

As we think about the next ten years, let's start with what great would look like in terms of professional progress. This will clearly depend on the stage of your career you are currently at, but try to think about what a great outcome would entail and then consider the steps you will need to take to achieve it. In all probability, the ideal outcome is not entirely in your own hands, but focusing on the things you *can* control is generally the best approach. You can waste a significant amount of energy if you focus on things that are beyond your control.

As part of this process, you may have to make difficult decisions. Perhaps your professional environment is not going to get you to where you want to be. Maybe, as you view the next ten years, being in your current career fills you with dread and makes you want to consider alternatives. Being deliberate in your thinking and proactive in your decision-making will help you to make change more successful and ensure you retain control of that change, rather than having it happening to you.

Your finances

What does great look like in your financial situation ten years from now? Professional progress and financial progress are linked, and it may be that achieving the career progress you want or making the career transition you need has an impact on your financial progress. This may be a compromise you are happy with or feel to be necessary.

The sense of fulfilment and happiness are about much more than just your bank balance, so you certainly shouldn't rule things out just because they potentially take you away from financial goals you have set. It may simply be that a readjustment of your financial goals is required. A nice house, car or holiday, for example, will only give you so much enjoyment. Meanwhile, doing work you truly love with people you like and have respect for will in most cases provide more happiness than material items.

When it comes to finance, flexibility and choice give more freedom. Something like reducing your mortgage so that you don't have a big debt can be an important step to take, as it will lead you towards financial freedom. Likewise, savings, investments and pensions can contribute to the sense that you are not forced to do the work you do, which can reduce stress. Make sure as well that, within the next ten years, you do some of the things you have always spoken about doing. We all have dreams and aspirations we might discuss with our partners, and it is important to tick off some of the things on your bucket list. Don't just leave these items for when you retire, because life is short and nobody knows what the future holds. We need to build in an element of living for today.

Looking at the next ten years, though, where would you like to be from a financial perspective?

For example, is there another property transaction to make, in either upsizing or downsizing? Do school fees or university costs start to ease off?

Overall, is the next ten years enough to take you to financial freedom? If not, that time frame can likely at least move you much further along the path. Even if you are at the start of your career now, within ten years your career will hopefully be established, and you will have been able to make some progress towards your long-term financial goals.

If you are in the fortunate position of having surplus income, how much do you allocate to living now and how much to future planning? Is this a question you have ever considered?

If, due to current commitments, you don't feel able to allocate as much to the future as you would like, don't worry; we all find ourselves in this position at times. Large mortgages, school fees and the general cost of living can put a strain on even those with really strong earnings. While you can't necessarily change existing commitments, though, you can commit to saving more of any increases you secure. This approach may not deliver progress as quickly as you would like, but your financial situation will gradually improve. In many cases those commitments that stop you from saving as much as you want to will gradually ease, and when that happens, you should immediately reallocate income to long-term savings, on the basis that you won't miss money you didn't have before.

Vision for beyond ten years

Now that you have looked at what you want to achieve over five and ten years, it is time to look towards the longer term. The ten-year vision is the last stepping stone towards the big future vision. For some that future vision is clear and immediately obvious, but that's not the case for everybody. Just because you don't have a detailed idea of what you would like the future to look like now doesn't mean you can't start planning ahead.

It is important to understand that life will throw things at you that you don't expect or that take you off course. This is entirely normal and happens to everybody, so you need to be flexible enough, in both your thinking and planning, to make adjustments. This might mean that ten years from now you have made far less progress than you had hoped. It could even mean that your previous plans and aspirations no longer appear achievable. These outcomes can be hard to accept, but they shouldn't mean you have to forgo the dream entirely.

It is likely you will just have to make some adjustments. While we all prefer not to make compromises, it is far better to make those that are necessary in advance, on your own terms, than having them forced upon you.

As the aspirations you have for your future are not yet a reality, once you mentally adjust, changes become part of your new plan, and you don't pay too much attention to the things you have decided against.

To start to form a clear idea in your mind of your long-term aspirations, consider these questions:

- How are all aspects of your life now; what does it feel like?

- What would a normal day be like ten years from now? What elements of these considerations make you excited when you think about them?
- What are the things you want to achieve with the time you have left?
- What will you regret if you don't do it at some point?
- What is that thing under the surface that you may never have mentioned to anybody, but which you secretly would love to do above all else?

Now is the time to bring these dreams and aspirations into the light. Airing them and discussing them with your partner will exponentially increase the likelihood that they will be achieved, however unrealistic they may feel now.

Not everyone has big dreams and ambitious plans – the future can be simpler. Being able to maintain the lifestyle they currently enjoy is a common aspiration for many of the legal professionals I work with. This is not always an easy thing to do, as many have worked hard and had significant incomes during their working life. They therefore need to save diligently to be able to support the comfortable lifestyle in retirement that their income generated during their careers.

Whatever your aspirations, now is the time to think carefully about how you want the future to look.

If achieving that future will require serious levels of capital, you will need to put in the hard work now to save it. If, on the other hand, your future aspirations are relatively modest, you will have more flexibility over time and, in particular, over how long you need to continue to work.

It can be helpful to go back to the categories we considered in Chapter 1 for the five-year vision and consider what a ten out of ten in each category would look like. Again, if there are areas that are not important to you, they can be ignored.

Does the plan you have come up with incorporate everything required to get to ten in all categories that are important to you?

Are there areas of compromise needed? If so, are you compromising in the least important areas?

Understanding what a great future for you and your family looks like is an important step. Just having that shared vision of the future can be a really powerful tool in planning your finances. In my experience, though, most people don't think about it, let alone discuss and agree it with their loved ones.

There are of course situations where it becomes clear that your vision of the future is not aligned with that of your partner, and as many marriages and relationships end in divorce or breakup, it would be naive to assume your relationship is immune to challenges. While a separation would undoubtedly have an impact on your financial planning and require some rethinking of your financial plan, having initially planned for the future will make it easier to change these plans when necessary.

Summary: Long-term planning

In this chapter we looked at how you can design the future you would like to see. We considered:

- What would be great progress over the next ten years and beyond
- How your vision for the short and medium term feeds into your long-term plans
- How you will be defined when you are no longer a lawyer, barrister or judge
- A fulfilling life when work is optional

Once you have reflected on all the points in this chapter, you will have a clear vision of a future you would like to build, over both the short and long term. While this vision and plan will inevitably change in due course, putting time into the first draft will help you to craft better future iterations that increase your motivation and excitement for the life ahead of you.

3

Understanding And Managing Debt

Just about everybody in the UK has some form of debt. While borrowing money can provide financial stability in the short and long term, it's likely we all understand financial freedom as being free from financial obligations. In this chapter I will look at beneficial ways to handle the debts you have or are likely to obtain.

Different types of debt

There are of course endless ways to borrow money and countless reasons for doing so. I will cover here the most common forms, some or all of which you likely already have, giving tips on how those debts can best be managed.

Student loans

For people who have relatively low levels of income, there is the prospect that student loans may not be paid in full, as they are eventually written off, with the point at which this happens depending on when the loan was originally started. This has resulted in certain financial journalists claiming that students should simply take out the loan and not worry too much about the interest rate, as in many cases the loan will be cancelled. While this may be true in many professions, if you have a long and successful career in law, it is unlikely to be the case.

The interest rate charged on student loans varies depending on when the loan was taken out, but all are charged at a rate of Retail Prices Index (RPI), with Plan 2 loans (undergraduate between 2012 and 2023) charged at up to RPI plus 3%. RPI is a measure of inflation, so the interest rate on Plan 2 loans is up to 3% above inflation (lower rates apply to those earning less than £51,245).

As with most forms of debt, it makes sense to consider repaying this debt early if you have surplus income, and it may be more beneficial to repay more than the minimum payments required. While I would not suggest repaying your student debt as a priority over buying a property or funding a pension or ISA, it may be prudent to repay your student loan before making less tax-efficient investments. It also makes sense to pay off the debt with the highest interest first to reduce overall cost, so credit cards would normally be the first priority, followed by personal loans or student debt, depending on interest rates.

Personal loans and credit cards

Personal loans and credit card obligations are unsecured forms of debt in which monthly payments of capital and interest are required. Rates on personal loans are generally higher than those on mortgages, while the interest rates on credit cards are some of the highest we see. This means it makes sense to pay off credit card debt before you start investing. The same can be true of personal loans, and a strategy to remove unsecured debt can be the first stage of long-term saving.

If you have a good credit rating, it is possible with credit cards sometimes to benefit from 0% interest rate introductory periods, in which you pay a small fee to transfer a balance from one card to another and then benefit from a period on which no interest is charged. In conjunction with this, you should look to increase your monthly payments to ensure the entire balance is paid off by the end of the interest-free period, either through regular payments or payments from distributions. If this is not possible, you may be able to find a second interest-free promotion on another card to repeat the process. While you should avoid taking out too many credit cards, if it takes a couple of periods to clear the debt in a cost-effective manner, additional cards can be helpful. The key here is not to spend additionally on the same credit card, as this will normally be charged at the standard (very high) rate of interest.

Once your credit card has been paid off, try not to use credit cards to provide you with credit. Instead, you can use one or two on which the balance is cleared fully every month for regular expenditure. There are two real advantages of this:

1. Many credit cards provide bonuses or incentives. This could be air miles, cashback or loyalty points with your preferred retailers.
2. Credit cards offer protection when you make purchases. This can be helpful if the retailer becomes insolvent between your order and delivery, or if you are subject to a scam.

Once you have paid off credit cards and personal loans, it is prudent generally to avoid debt other than in mortgages. One exception to this can be interest-free credit, which can allow you to spread the cost of significant purchases over a period of time. If using this type of credit, make sure you repay fully before any interest becomes payable, and don't borrow any amounts that you won't be able to repay before interest is chargeable, as typically the interest payable if you exceed the interest-free period is relatively high.

Mortgages

Typically, mortgages are a form of long-term debt, with interest rates fixed over a shorter period of two to five years.

When buying your first property, you probably used a repayment mortgage, which is a very sensible approach. Each month your repayments are made up of both interest and capital, with the capital element increasing over time as the debt becomes smaller and therefore the interest lower.

If you take out a large mortgage on a more expensive property, you can find that the monthly repayments are significant, sometimes exceeding your monthly drawings. I have seen occasions when partners have therefore elected to take the mortgage on an interest-only basis, meaning that they pay only the interest on the loan on a monthly basis. They then use distributions to repay capital, which in turn reduces interest payments. They continue on this basis until they have reduced the mortgage to a more manageable level, during which time we tend to restrict investments to only those areas in which tax benefits are provided – benefits that would otherwise be lost. Most mortgage deals allow a 10% repayment of capital per annum without penalty, which often provides enough scope for some investment alongside mortgage reduction. Sometimes, though, I will advise clients to build up cash over the final year or two of the mortgage deal so they can make a further capital reduction before locking into another mortgage deal.

While it is normal to repay mortgage debt over twenty-five years, paying it off early and quickly not only saves a significant expenditure on interest but also provides considerable flexibility when it comes to future planning. If you still have a large monthly commitment to mortgage payments as you get closer to retirement, it can restrict your ability to retire early or to take on a different, less remunerative role. Paying off debt early provides greater financial freedom and so is a good approach to take.

It is still more beneficial to fund future investments alongside debt reduction if possible, as the value of investments is extracted over the long term. For those with significant surplus income, though, a more aggressive approach to mortgage repayment is beneficial. With the clients I work with, we tend to focus heavily on debt reduction in the early years of the large mortgage, just until they get it down to a level they feel comfortable with, before taking a more balanced approach.

The use of an offset mortgage can also be beneficial. With an offset mortgage you have a savings account linked to the mortgage, and any savings you have offset the mortgage interest. For example, if you had £1 million in the savings element and £1 million of outstanding mortgage, no interest would be payable. This can work well because interest on savings is subject to taxation, but interest payments on debt (other than business finance) are not allowable, so you pay the interest from taxed income but pay tax on any savings income. An offset mortgage can work extremely well for barristers or partners at firms that don't maintain a tax reserve, as the money you set aside for taxation can be used to reduce your mortgage payments.

Summary: Understanding and managing debt

In this chapter we have considered the various forms of debt and covered:

- What to do about student debt
- Why personal loans and credit cards are not necessarily the best way to borrow
- How mortgages work and some approaches to consider for paying them off

You should now have a good understanding, both of any debt you have now and of any future debt commitments you might take on.

PART TWO

R – REVIEW YOUR CURRENT SITUATION

Before you start to build your long-term financial plan, you need to understand your current position. In this section we will consider any existing financial products you hold, to understand whether they continue to be appropriate for use to achieve your financial objectives. We will also discuss other financial products that may be used within your financial plan.

We will consider the importance of aligning your planning with your values and ensuring that you focus on the things that really matter to you rather than on those you think you should be doing.

4
Your Current Reality

This chapter will guide you through assessing and evaluating any financial products you use and assets you hold. This will give you vital information on the start of your journey towards financial freedom.

Taking stock – financial perspective

Now that you have something of an idea of where you want to get to, let's look at any financial assets and investments you have accumulated so far. This is often a melting pot of different plans and policies that have been taken out at various points and may have since been largely forgotten about.

For people that have spent time abroad, the melting pot can include a series of foreign financial products for which you have limited information. Bringing order to this can appear to be an impossible task, or it may be that you have very little to organise and are worried whether you should have accumulated more financial assets than you have. In either case, it is not something to worry about. As we work through the stages, you will have an opportunity to build up all of the financial assets you require and to understand the financial products you already have. This will allow you to decide what to keep and what no longer serves a purpose.

If you have no existing financial products, it simply means you are starting with a blank sheet of paper and can ensure that all of your financial decisions are informed ones. When looking at existing holdings, take a moment to consider which categories apply to your assets and make a list of financial products and their values arranged by the types outlined in the next section of this chapter.

Protection

The term *protection* always makes me think of sleek-haired men with pencil moustaches, in 1930s suits, demanding money to prevent a shop or bar coming to harm.

In this case, though, we are considering insurance policies that will provide a payout if a certain event takes place. While we will cover protection in more detail later, at this stage I want to highlight the main types so that you know what they are as you sort through your paperwork.

The most common form of financial protection is life insurance, which provides a lump sum in the event of your death. This insurance is often taken out in conjunction with a mortgage and linked to the mortgage term. Sometimes the amount of life insurance that is due to be paid to your beneficiaries reduces as your mortgage is paid off, and in other cases it stays level throughout the term of the insurance.

Alongside life insurance (and sometimes integrated within the same policy) is critical illness insurance, which pays a lump sum if you are diagnosed with a serious illness.

Other policies include income protection (or permanent health insurance, as it was previously known), which provides income if you are unable to work; and sickness, accident and redundancy cover, which, as the name suggests, provides income for a period of up to twelve months. There may also be benefits provided through your employer or within the partnership structure.

Savings

This category includes all bank deposits, ie sums in your current account and any savings accounts as well as cash ISAs. It would also include any National Savings products such as Premium Bonds or Savings Certificates.

Included here also would be any longer-term savings such as term deposits, which are fixed-term savings accounts. These typically provide higher levels of interest in exchange for tying money up for a longer period.

Investments

Here you would need to consider anything in which the value of the holding can fluctuate and is therefore not fixed.

These holdings are typically intended to be longer-term investments and could include investments in ISAs, individual company shares, investment bonds, unit trusts, investment trusts and endowment policies. We look in more detail at different types of financial products and investments later in the book, so don't worry at this stage if you are not sure which label applies to the assets you have.

Property

This is probably the area people are most comfortable with, and it would be helpful for you to make a note of property assets held and then to include within your notes details of the current value of these assets.

(Websites such as Zoopla can be used to find approximate values of residential property.) This may include assets other than your home, such as a holiday home or commercial property.

I would suggest the property value is viewed as the sale price that could be achieved if a quick sale was required, to avoid putting too optimistic a value on your property. We are not selling at this stage, so the estimated value is not that crucial.

Pensions

As the name suggests, this category is about retirement products. There are a wide range of different types, which are generally grouped into two types of policies:

1. **Defined contribution policies:** A pension value is built up and is then used to provide retirement income.
2. **Defined benefit policies:** A level of pension income is provided, which is normally linked to salary and term of service.

Defined benefit pensions are less common these days and have never been widely used by legal practices. The two defined benefit schemes I come across most often are the Judicial Pension Scheme and the Civil Service Pension Scheme. The pensions available to most individuals in the legal profession tend to be defined contribution schemes.

Debt

This category typically comprises mortgages and student loans, but might also include personal loans or credit cards.

Some individuals may also hold partnership loans, which relate to capital contributions to the partnership. I would not include these at this stage, as the expectation is that your share of partnership capital will be sufficient to pay off the partnership loan when you leave the partnership.

Evaluating existing holdings

Once you have pulled together all of your financial information and categorised it, you will have a clearer picture of your assets (savings, investments and property) and liabilities (debt) as well as information about any insurance and your pension provision. At this stage, it is important simply to know what your liabilities are rather than passing judgement or considering what you might do about them.

Let's look now in more detail at what your existing financial products are and what you require.

Savings

As a general rule, you should keep at least six months' worth of expenditure in short-term cash, ie in an instant-access bank account, as an emergency fund. This ensures you have sufficient funds available to deal with anything unexpected. While that could relate to simple things like the washing machine needing to be replaced, it could also cover redundancy or ill health. Some prefer to keep more in cash, and that is not necessarily the wrong thing to do. An allocation of 10–25% of your wealth in cash can make sense, particularly if you are either less comfortable with investment risk or are in the fortunate position of not needing to take much investment risk.

Two of the most important things to consider here are whether the interest rate you are getting on your cash holdings is competitive and how exposed you are to the failure of a bank or savings institution. With short-term cash, convenience is more important than returns, so I wouldn't necessarily suggest moving to an alternative account that is difficult to access just to get a better interest rate. It can still make sense, though, to shop around for a decent rate.

With larger or longer-term cash holdings, convenience tends to be less important as you are unlikely to need to access funds very quickly. Looking for attractive interest rates can make sense, and a number of comparison sites provide access to details of the best savings rates.

Many of the better rates are offered by banks that are not household names, and if you are considering a less well-known bank, I would suggest ensuring they are covered by the Financial Services Compensation Scheme (most comparison sites include details of this) and sticking within the compensation limits. Also consider National Savings & Investments, which won't generally be included within comparison sites but whose rates are provided on their website.

Insurance

With life insurance, the first step is to consider the level of cover you need. This involves looking not only at the cover you have taken out but also any provided by your firm, if applicable. You should then consider the following questions:

- Will the mortgage be paid off if my partner or I die?
- Is there enough cover in place to provide for our family if either of us dies?
- Would I receive any income if I were ill or unable to work?
- Do I have a lump sum available, in case I suffer a serious illness?

The answers to these questions should give you a good idea of the level of cover you require, and you can then compare this with the cover you have to plug any shortfalls or potentially remove cover that is not required. Be aware when removing cover that it can be more expensive in many cases to put new cover in place. Additionally, it may be impossible to reinstate cover if you have suffered an illness since the start of your policy, so you need to think carefully before cancelling it.

Investment

There are two stages of looking at your investment holdings.

1. Providers and costs

This is easy to manage across a small number of providers, but you may have taken out a wide range of products over the years, perhaps due to a suggestion from a friend or because you met a financial adviser at a time when you had some spare cash and they sold you a product.

You will need to consider the charges on the investments that you have. Do they vary between fund holdings?

As a very general rule, if you are managing the assets yourself, the cost should be no more than 1% per annum (and it can sometimes be much lower). If you have an adviser, the total cost should be no more than 2% per annum (and again, this can also be much lower). If you do have an adviser, you may want to evaluate whether they are helping you in all areas of planning your financial future or just telling you which investments to buy.

2. How your assets are invested

I'll cover this in more depth in Chapter 9, but for now it is important to note that the mix of investments you hold is aligned to your long-term objectives and risk tolerance.

If your portfolio does well when markets are up but scares the life out of you when markets go down, you may have more risk exposure than you are comfortable with. At the other end of the scale, if you are constantly frustrated with the performance of your portfolio and always feel it should be doing better, you may need a little more exposure to investment risk.

Pensions

Depending on how extensive your work history is, this could be the hardest or easiest area to review. As most people in the legal profession will not have defined benefit pension schemes, those will not be covered here. The one exception is the Judicial Pension Scheme, which is no longer a registered pension scheme. If you are lucky enough to be in this scheme, the chances are that you will be able to draw the judicial pension after you retire, which is very likely to be the best option for you.

With a defined contribution pension scheme, there are a few questions to check whether they are fit for purpose:

- Are funds invested in line with your needs (level of investment risk, the geographical spread of investments), and have any ethical considerations that are important to you been included in the investment selection?
- Can you make adjustments to the investment selection?
- Are the charges competitive? The annual fee should be less than 1% (if no financial advice is included).
- Do you have multiple polices that could be combined?

If you are looking to make changes or wish to replace existing pensions, charges and flexibility tend to be the main drivers of change. For example, if you have one pension with low charges and a good fund range, this would make a good candidate for a consolidation of other pensions.

One area where you need to take care is around policies taken out before 1989, as they could benefit from guaranteed annuity rates. This is because they provide favourable rates at which lifetime income can be provided and are normally much higher than current rates. If you have guaranteed annuity rates, it would probably be worthwhile you seeking independent financial advice before doing anything with the policy, as you could be at risk of giving up valuable benefits. The same can be true if you have any form of occupational pension scheme that started before April 2006, as there could be benefits in leaving the pension where it is. As with defined benefit pension schemes, most law firms tended to use group personal pensions (GPPs), which are not occupational pension schemes. These types of schemes will be rare; however, there may be some around, and individuals who worked outside of law firms may have been in these types of schemes. As a general rule, if your pension has the words *personal pension* in the name, it should be fine to consolidate it, but anything like *retirement annuity*, *retirement benefit scheme* or *company pension scheme* may require investigation by a financial adviser before you consider any changes.

Summary: Your current reality

In this chapter we considered all the financial products you may have picked up until now. We covered:

- Categorising financial products
- Understanding what you currently hold

- Evaluating the suitability of your existing holdings
- Considering how any investments are allocated between different asset classes

After this chapter you should have a clear idea of the financial products you hold, and a neat summary of them which will be extremely helpful to your future planning. You will also now have some idea whether they remain suitable for you or require attention.

5

Understanding Financial Products And Investments

Financial products are the engine that drives you towards your goals and, as such, they are important but functional. Many financial professionals spend all of their time focusing on financial products, whereas I see them more as a necessary tool to achieve the most important things in life. This chapter will give you a solid understanding of the main financial products and which ones are likely to be most beneficial to you.

The list below isn't intended to be exhaustive, and I have avoided any 'weird and wonderful' products. This is mainly because most of us do not need overly complex or expensive solutions, however much our bankers or financial advisers might try to convince us otherwise!

Protection

Insurance protects you against things that could go wrong and is therefore a vital part of long-term planning. There are a wide range of products available, but I am going to focus on the main ones here. We will look at how we apply them later, but this section gives a brief summary of the main options.

Life insurance

Life insurance, which provides your beneficiaries with a lump sum if you die, is typically based on a fixed term. If taken out when you are young, the premiums are quite cheap because the likelihood of death is low. The two main types are:

1. **Level term assurance:** Level of cover remains constant throughout the term
2. **Decreasing term assurance:** Level of cover reduces over time, typically in line with repayment of a mortgage

Family income benefit

With this type of policy, rather than paying out a lump sum in the case of the policy holder's death, the plan pays out a monthly tax-free amount, based on an annual calculation. This can be ideal, for example to cover the cost of childcare or to help a surviving spouse to bring up children.

The cost of a family income benefit policy is lower than a term assurance policy because the potential payout that could apply reduces for each year that you survive, as monthly payments are paid only until the end of the policy term. Another advantage is that the partner left behind will receive a monthly tax-free payment, which is usually easier to manage than a lump sum, which would need to be invested to provide an annual income.

Critical illness cover

This is insurance that pays out a lump sum on diagnosis of a serious illness (normally requiring you to live for thirty days after diagnosis). Critical illness cover can be used to cover living expenses or other costs such as home alterations if you are no longer able to work.

Some policies pay out graduated amounts depending on the severity of the illness. As serious illnesses are unfortunately fairly common, the cost of this cover can be high, but it is a valuable protection to have in place.

Income protection

Income protection (sometimes known as permanent health insurance) provides a replacement for a proportion of your income if you are unable to work for any reason. Although cheaper policies sometimes have a maximum payout period of one or two years, my preference in this area is for policies that run until retirement. This is because if you need to claim on this type of policy, the insurance cannot be cancelled in the future, and your income payments can continue until the end of the term. You therefore have the security that you will still receive some income to support your lifestyle if you can't return to work.

The monthly income that can be provided by the policy is restricted to a proportion of your earned income, and the tax treatment of benefits depends on whether the policy is provided by your employer (income is taxable) or taken out yourself (income paid tax-free).

Savings

There are a range of different options for savings, with the main types of accounts outlined below.

Savings account

A savings account is typically separate from your current account, although the two are sometimes linked. It would normally pay a little more interest than your current account (which typically pays no interest) and offers instant access, meaning you can take money out of the account at any time without a penalty of interest. Interest rates are widely published, and you should be able to easily move between accounts. Some of the private banks offer quite competitive cash rates, whereas high street bank rates tend to be fairly low.

Term deposit

This is a fixed-term savings account where, in exchange for you tying up your capital for a set period of time, a higher rate of interest is provided. Generally, the longer you are happy to tie up the capital, the higher the interest rate. However, a long-term deposit exposes you to the risk that interest rates may increase, making the rate you agreed to less competitive.

There are also notice accounts, which, rather than tying up funds for a fixed term, require a certain amount of notice before funds can be withdrawn. While both options can be attractive, these accounts are more restrictive than savings accounts, and you should think carefully whether you will require the money during the term.

Cash ISA (individual savings account)

A cash ISA is one into which you can deposit cash and pay no tax on the interest. By providing an annual amount (£20,000 at the time of writing) that can be saved on which no tax is paid or interest generated, cash ISAs were established to encourage people to save more. You can purchase instant access and term deposit cash ISAs. See also the 'Investment ISA' section later in this chapter.

You can transfer between cash and investment ISAs at any time, as well as between different cash or investment ISAs. If you withdraw money, though, you may not be able to put it back into the ISA unless it is a flexible ISA, which allows you to pay money back in, provided you do so within the same tax year.

If you want to move between ISAs, for example to benefit from a better rate, it makes sense to do so through a transfer of the ISA rather than by withdrawing the money, as this will ensure that the ISA tax treatment is preserved.

Lifetime ISA

At the time of writing, Lifetime ISAs use an element of the normal ISA allowance. They can be established by those between the ages of eighteen and forty and allow an investment of up to £4,000 into an ISA, on which a 25% government top-up is added. Although a lifetime ISA must be established before the age of forty, you can continue to fund and receive the top-up until the age of fifty. The condition to this top-up is that the funds can only be withdrawn to fund a first property purchase (with a purchase price of no more than £450,000) or after the age of sixty. If you withdraw funds for any other reason, a penalty of 25% of the lifetime ISA fund value will apply. As the penalty is applied to the entire lifetime ISA value, it is generally more than the bonus that was provided.

Financial Services Compensation Scheme

When holding money in savings or term deposit accounts, it can be worth considering how secure your bank is. To provide confidence in banks, there is a compensation scheme that at the time of writing protects up to £120,000 of savings – or £240,000 for joint accounts – in any bank with a UK banking licence. Be aware that more than one bank within the same banking group can share the same banking licence, so you would need to check who owns the banks behind each of your deposits.

The compensation scheme is very helpful, particularly in securing more competitive rates on deposits at smaller, less established banks. There is certainly an argument that you should keep all deposits within the compensation scheme limits, ensuring that you are never impacted by the failure of a bank. Others take a more pragmatic view, feeling it is unlikely that a major UK bank would be allowed to fail (as was perhaps demonstrated in the 2008 global financial crisis). There is a relatively simple solution, however, in National Savings.

National Savings and Investments (NS&I)

NS&I are a government-owned savings organisation, which is used as a means to raise money for government spending, alongside the sale of gilts. NS&I are given a target amount of fundraising by government, and depending on the amount that needs to be raised, they will increase or reduce interest rates to control deposit flows.

The big advantage to National Savings over other savings accounts is that because they are government-owned, your capital is protected. In the event of a default by the UK Government, there is the possibility you could lose money, but that risk is seen as quite remote (and as the government stands behind the Financial Services Compensation Scheme, one would assume that this could also be at risk, in the event of insolvency of the UK Government). This allows you to hold more than the compensation limit within NS&I, with no increased default risk.

Premium bonds

NS&I offer a range of products, most of which are very similar to instant access or term deposits. One of their products, which is slightly different, is Premium Bonds. These are instant-access accounts on which prizes are paid rather than interest. These prizes are paid tax-free and are awarded twice a month, via a random number selector called ERNIE. There are generally two prizes of £1 million and over five million prizes in total, ranging from £1 million down to £25. At the time of writing, the overall prize fund is 3.3% per annum, and the chances of winning are quoted as 23,000 to 1.[3]

Given the number of prizes and the frequency of drawing, one would expect a return on average of around the 3.3% prize fund mark, although there is an element of luck, and your actual return could be between £0 and £1 million for each £1 bond.

Investments

Investments, as opposed to savings, offer no certainty of nominal value, which is why some people shy away from investing. The purpose of investments is to provide higher returns over the longer term.

In many cases investments can be better at protecting real values (ie inflation-adjusted amounts) over the longer term, which is a perceived weakness of savings. Interest rates are set by central banks and are not linked to inflation, meaning that while cash provides a protection of nominal value, in real terms it often falls in value. As with other financial areas, there are a vast range of financial products. It is not my intention to cover every type of financial product

3 NS&I, 'Interest rates: Premium Bonds prize fund rate' (no date), www.nsandi.com/interest-rates, accessed 9 April 2026

here but to give details of some of the main ones you may come across.

Investment ISA and lifetime ISA

The annual ISA allowance (and, if eligible, the lifetime ISA allowance) can be used to invest in non-cash assets. All investment returns are provided free from taxation, meaning that your investments can grow on an ongoing basis without tax deductions. A major advantage of this tax efficiency is the ability to make tax-free withdrawals from your ISA at any time, although any lifetime ISA element will be subject to the same restrictions as outlined above (see 'Lifetime ISA' earlier in this chapter).

I generally advise clients to use ISAs for long-term savings and, in particular, to help to provide income after retirement. Given the long-term nature of this objective, investment ISAs rather than cash ISAs – are more appropriate. This is because we would expect higher returns from investments over the longer term than from cash. (There would be no sense in taking investment risk if we didn't expect stronger returns over the long term.) As the tax saving is provided on the investment return generated rather than on the invested capital, it makes sense to apply the tax saving to assets on which we expect the highest return.

With clients who have surplus income to save, I recommend them making use of their ISA allowance each year, as over time this can build up to a significant sum. There are a number of investors who, having combined strong investment returns and with consistent use of the allowance, now hold more than £1 million in ISAs. Having a sizeable capital sum on which you can draw tax-free income or capital can be valuable in later life, particularly in maximising your income without being subject to higher levels of taxation.

General investment and non-ISA investment

While the ISA regime is valuable and allows funds to be saved in a tax-efficient manner, for many successful legal professionals the allowance is insufficient for the amounts they need to save. They will therefore need to save outside of an ISA, and the product that is normally used for this is known in the industry as a *general investment account* (GIA). This essentially means that the investment is not held within an ISA or any other structure.

You can invest in a wide range of investment holdings, and anything that can be held in an ISA could also be held in a GIA. The only difference is the tax treatment, as with these holdings you will be subject to income and/or capital gains tax on investment returns.

Income tax is charged each year on any interest or dividends generated. The income is added to your other income and taxed at the progressive tax rates that apply to your earned income. Interest is generally paid from fixed income holdings which are debt investments.

In the case of investments into companies, if income is provided, it generally comes in the form of dividends, ie a share of a company's profits. Because these profits have already been subject to corporation tax before they are paid to you, dividends are taxed at slightly lower rates. There is also a small dividend allowance, meaning you can receive a small amount of income before dividends are subject to tax deductions.

The other way companies provide investment returns is via increases in their share prices. When you eventually sell shares, you will be taxed on the difference between what you paid for them and what you sold them for. This is called *capital gains tax*, and you again have an allowance before any tax is payable. The rates of capital gains tax are lower than income tax rates, but they are again linked to your other income in calculating which rate you pay. As tax rates and allowances change periodically, I have purposely not stated the current rates; this is something that is easy to look up.

We have seen that non-ISA holdings are less tax efficient than ISAs, but they can still be used to provide long-term savings and, when required, can be used to provide valuable income and capital when it is needed. A strategy I use with most of my clients is arranging for them to fund a GIA alongside an ISA during their working lives. Once they retire, we sell from the GIA to continue to fund the ISA, thereby continuing to move funds into a more tax-efficient environment, even when a client no longer has surplus earned income.

Investment bond

Investment bonds can be UK-based or offshore, and they are investments that are subject to insurance rules. This means they need to include an element of insurance, although this is typically very limited. These products allow you to withdraw up to 5% of your original capital each year without immediate tax liability. This allowance is cumulative, so if you take nothing in the first five years, for example, you would be able to withdraw 30% in year six, representing the 5% allowance for all six years.

Any withdrawals in excess of this are called chargeable events and are subject to income tax at your marginal tax rate. With a UK investment bond, basic rate tax is paid within the structure, so additional tax liabilities are limited to a higher rate or an additional rate of tax. With an offshore investment bond, no tax is paid on an ongoing basis, so tax applies to all withdrawals except for non-tax payers or very low rate taxpayers.

Investment bonds can be helpful within trust planning and have some valuable features, such as the ability to make withdrawals without immediate tax liabilities and the ability to switch funds without tax charge. These make them worthwhile if ISAs have been fully funded and you already have a significant portfolio of assets that are subject to capital gains tax. While I would often use this structure with clients, on a layered basis after ISAs and GIAs, most non-advised clients tend to stick with ISAs and GIAs, but if you have had a previous adviser, you may hold an investment bond.

Venture capital trust (VCT) and enterprise investment scheme (EIS)

Both of these investments receive tax incentives to encourage investment in smaller companies. As they are investments in small, normally early-stage companies, they are much higher risk than more traditional holdings, and I have seen many situations in which the losses from investments have far outweighed the tax breaks provided.

A VCT is an investment into a fund that holds a portfolio of shares in small companies. Tax relief is generally provided quickly, and many VCTs provide dividends, which are paid tax-free and can be a valuable source of tax-free income. Changes to investment rules for VCT make investing into income-generative holdings more difficult now, although VCTs are able to keep existing holdings.

An EIS is an investment into a single company. Many promoters of EIS investments package them into small portfolios, as for most people, the risk associated with investment into a single company is too high. An EIS provides loss relief on investments that don't perform, as well as having inheritance tax planning benefits.

Both of these investments are much higher risk than other investment types and would therefore ideally form only a small element of a portfolio, and even then only for individuals who are comfortable with the risk involved. The risk means it is likely that at least some of the companies within a portfolio will fail, but provided others perform well, they can be an attractive investment.

There is a further investment option in this area, the Seed Enterprise Investment Scheme (SEIS), which invests into even smaller companies and generates higher tax breaks but poses an even higher risk. Given the additional investment risk, an SEIS is suitable for only a relatively small group of investors.

Pensions

As mentioned in Chapter 4, there are two types of pensions:

1. **Defined benefit:** The pension you receive is a proportion of your salary when working.

2. **Defined contribution:** A pension fund is built up and used to provide an income in retirement.

In this book we will focus on defined contribution pensions, as very few people in the legal profession are members of defined benefit pension schemes.

The advantage of saving in a pension is that you receive tax relief on any contributions made to the scheme. The funds within the pension then grow tax-free, and although you are subject to income tax on withdrawals, you can normally take 25% of the pension fund as a tax-free lump sum.

If you are an associate, the firm will generally make contributions for you into the pension scheme of their choice. Many schemes make contributions through salary sacrifice, meaning your personal contributions are made as employer contributions through a reduction in your salary. For example, if your salary is £80,000 and your pension contributions are 5% of your salary, your salary would be reduced to £76,000, with the £4,000 pension contribution being made as an employer pension contribution. Firms do this because it generates a saving in National Insurance contributions. Typically, firms allow you to keep the (smaller) employee saving while they keep the employer saving, making it a win for both sides.

If you become a partner or are a barrister, you will be expected to make your own pension contributions. In some cases you can use a pension scheme from a previous employer or set up a new pension policy. It will then be up to you how much you contribute each year to the pension.

Annual allowance

Because of the valuable tax relief provided to the pension scheme, there is a limit to the amount that can be contributed to a pension. This is called the annual allowance, and it is currently set at the lower of either 100% of your earnings or £60,000 per annum. However, provided you have sufficient earned income, you can make use of any annual allowance you haven't used over the previous three years. This allows you to make a larger pension contribution if you have made smaller contributions in previous tax years.

I use this tactic often when working with corporate lawyers who have recently been promoted to partner, as they typically have an opportunity to make use of their higher earnings (before their expenditure has significantly increased) to make larger pension contributions that they may not be able to make in the future. The reason they would not be able to make larger contributions in the future is that the annual allowance is reduced for those earning more than £260,000 per annum. The calculation of tapered annual allowance can be somewhat complex, as there is both a threshold income calculation and an adjusted income calculation, which have slightly different methods of calculation.

Both threshold and adjusted income would include all remuneration from work (whether employed or self-employed) as well as savings income, dividend income, rental income and any income from pensions or trusts. This is not an exhaustive list, and if you are in any doubt, you may wish to get advice from an accountant. Some losses can be offset against this income. The most common are gifts of shares or property to charity (not including Gift Aid), losses from some unquoted shares (in particular EIS holdings covered previously) and some business losses (for those in the legal profession, these are probably partnership losses).

Threshold income is then total income less pension contributions, although any salary sacrifice arrangements that started after 2015 would also be added back into the calculation. Threshold income is relevant only if it is below £200,000, because if the threshold income is less than £200,000, regardless of adjusted income, no tapering of the annual allowance will apply.

Adjusted income adds back employer pension contributions, which would not be relevant for partners and barristers as they are generally self-employed, but this could be relevant for high-earning associates or employed lawyers. If your adjusted income is more than £260,000, your annual allowance will be reduced by £1 for every £2 that you are over this level. This means that if your adjusted income exceeds £340,000, your annual allowance will reach the minimum of £10,000 per annum.

I have used the limits and rates that apply at the time of writing. These can be subject to change, and it would be worthwhile to check current rates before taking any action.

These rules mean that many high-earning lawyers and barristers are very much restricted on the amount that can be saved in a pension. In addition to making pension savings, they also need to consider other methods to save for retirement, which mostly involves using the investments covered earlier in this chapter.

There is a further restriction around pensions, which relates to the level of lump sum that can be provided tax-free. This is generally 25% of the value of your pension, but there is an upper restriction on the total amount that can be paid that is exempt from tax deductions. The rules we currently have in place have occurred as a result of the abolition of another set of rules, the *lifetime allowance*, which used to restrict the total amount that could be saved in a pension.

The current rules state that while you can save as much as you want into a pension, the most that can be paid out as a tax-free lump sum across all your pensions and over your entire lifetime is £268,275. This amount is not index linked and will therefore lose value in real terms over time. A range of different protections have been available at different times, meaning some individuals have the ability to have a larger lump sum. If you have pension protection, you may need to seek professional advice if you need assistance.

One of the real potential benefits of contributing to a pension arises in cases where tax relief is provided at a higher rate than your tax rate in retirement. This can mean you receive tax relief of 45% on your pension contributions and pay tax at a rate of 20% or 40% on the income you take from the pension in retirement. The benefit of this uplift, together with the tax-free lump sum and tax-free growth while the funds are invested, mean that investing in a pension remains one of the best ways to fund retirement. However, care can be needed to remain within contribution limits. If your pension fund will exceed £1,073,100, you need to be aware that no further tax-free amount will be accrued, which if you are likely to remain subject to the same level of tax in retirement, could make it more beneficial to invest into other areas.

Summary: Understanding financial products and investments

We have now considered all of the financial products you are likely to come across. While this list is not exhaustive and there are always new types of products launched, we have covered the bulk of financial products that are available in the UK market. We considered:

- Insurance products that support you and your family should you suffer ill health or die
- Savings products for emergency or short-term capital requirements
- The financial compensation scheme, what it is, how it works and the limits of protection
- Investment products, with a range of different options, including tax-incentivised options
- Pensions

With this understanding of products, you have new building blocks that will be used within your financial plan.

6

Values – Follow Your Own Path

Values are the essential beliefs and principles that guide our behaviours and opinions. They provide a framework through which we view the world, and they are responsible for our actions, which also have a big impact on our feelings. When we take actions that are in line with our values, we feel a heightened sense of satisfaction. When we do things that are counter to our values (which we all do at times), we can feel a sense of unease or unhappiness, even if the results of those actions appear successful.

Why values are important

Because values play a big part in happiness and the enjoyment we gain from our endeavours and achievements, they are extremely important when we consider planning an ideal future. While some people can clearly and easily identify their values, if this is not something you have considered before, it can be difficult to know where to start or what your values might be.

There are a number of methods you can use to clarify your values, including an online exercise that will take you through a values clarification process to give you a good starting point for understanding your values. Once you have clarity on the those that resonate most for you, it will help to ensure that your future planning is aligned to your values, which will in turn increase the possibility of living a fulfilling life in the future. If you are planning your ideal future life, you should at least make sure it is fulfilling!

If, for example, one of your values is helpfulness – that you like to be able to help people and this is something your work entails – it would make sense to consider how you can satisfy this value once you retire. Could you, for example, use your legal training within a charity or sporting organisation? Would a non-executive role provide you with that reward?

Another area in which values can be important can be around the products you use and the investments you hold. For example, if environmental considerations are important to you, as they are for many, it doesn't make sense to profit from the success of companies that are some of the heaviest polluters.

Similarly, if honesty is one of your core values, it wouldn't make sense for you to invest in companies who are found to mislead customers or regulators. Over recent years, *socially responsible investment* (SRI) has become a buzzword in the investment industry, with regulation requiring investment companies to make clear what areas they invest in and the positive impact that they have. This is intended to tackle greenwashing, in which investments have been marketed using the terms SRI or ESG (environmental, social and governance), while investing into companies that don't really fit this description.

For many, ensuring that the investments they hold conform to their beliefs is as important as the investment returns generated, and fortunately there are now many strong options in these areas, allowing investments to be aligned to values, while still working towards long-term goals.

MARY'S APPROACH

Mary is passionate about conservation and protecting our planet. It is one of her strongest values and something she thinks about every day. The health of the planet is more important to her than her own needs, and she believes we all need to adjust the way we live to minimise (and hopefully reverse) the damage we have done to our planet and all living things. She doesn't drive a car, she won't take plane journeys, and she runs community environmental projects in her spare time.

Mary's pensions were held in company default options that her current and previous employer had selected for her. Her employment, although well paid, was not really aligned to her values, and she felt that she was in conflict with the ethos and approach of the company, which made her working environment challenging for her.

When we started to work together, we discussed long-term goals and ambitions, and Mary's passions came through strongly. We considered what would bring the aspects of her life into line with her values and identified a few areas where she could consider making some change, including around the funds her pension was invested in. We agreed to use a combination of investments, which excluded some of the worst-performing companies and avoided investment into areas such as mining and oil. We then agreed to invest a relatively small percentage, due to the high risks, into impact investments, in which companies were seeking to bring to market new technologies that would have a positive environmental impact.

When we spoke about Mary's work, it was clear she was not feeling fulfilled in her current role. We spoke about future possibilities, and one thing she wanted to consider was using her skills, within her profession, to help people improve their environmental impact. Mary had an idea for a company she could build in that space. Although this was something she felt excited about, she didn't quite feel ready to take that step. Instead, she found a role at another firm in which she was involved in considering the environmental impact of all of the work that the firm does. The new role is hard work and extremely demanding, but because it is aligned to the values that are most important to Mary, she loves it and is thriving much more than when she was at her previous firm.

Tailoring your approach to you

It is important that you adjust your plan to fit in with an approach you are comfortable with. When you get to consider the amounts of capital to hold in certain areas and the level of financial security that should be maintained, it is fine if you feel you need a little more security or, within reason, that less security is OK. A key element of the planning is to build financial well-being, and that is impossible if you are taking actions that are not sufficient to meet your need for security, although this need is different for each of us.

Likewise, when we look at investment risk, it may be that you have a higher or lower risk tolerance than others, and this will require a slight adjustment to the investment approach to ensure that it works for you. If you take on too much risk, you will find yourself becoming anxious every time you see a newspaper article suggesting markets are set to fall, or when the news reports record falls in stock markets. This type of anxiety can cause significant, unnecessary worry. In this situation, having less exposure to higher-risk assets would normally reduce your anxiety, as knowing that only part of your wealth is linked to these areas and much more is unaffected by market movements would provide sufficient reassurance to ease any concerns.

Conversely, if you feel disappointed when you see markets providing strong growth and look at your own more modest returns, it could be a sign you could take more investment risk. Before doing so, though, I would suggest also considering your feelings when your investments fall in value, as is inevitable with stocks and shares. Nobody enjoys losing money, but provided you can remain philosophical during these periods, more investment risk might be appropriate.

Often it takes experience of different market conditions to understand how you truly feel about investment risk. Generally, the first time you go through a market correction where you have a decent amount of a capital built up is the hardest. It is at this point where, if you do become nervous about markets and investments, fear will come to the fore. Every fibre of your body may be telling you to sell everything and accept that investing is not for you, but here you need to hold firm, sit on your hands and generally do nothing. If you are investing regularly, carry on doing so. If you invest from distributions, you should continue to make the investments as planned if at all possible, although it's OK if you feel you have to pause on this occasion. What you really must avoid is selling out and crystallising the loss; once the money is returned to cash, it could take many years to recover the losses.

I add some of the most value in my work with clients at these times, providing reassurance and ensuring that they stay the course and don't panic. Often once markets have recovered (which they have always historically done, although there is, of course, no guarantee this will always be the case), we would review things together and consider whether less risk would be better. For many people, after they have then seen the recovery, they feel more comfortable to face the next market correction, and the experience has prepared them and increased their resilience and risk tolerance. Having said that, while having a 100% equity approach may offer the potential for the strongest long-term returns, the corrections could be quite extreme and are likely to be more than most would be comfortable with.

Summary: Values – follow your own path

We have considered values and ensuring that your plan is aligned to your own requirements rather than something somebody has told you should be done. In this chapter we covered:

- The importance of considering your values within financial planning

- Understanding your own preferences and using them in your planning
- Considering the level of investment risk you are comfortable with

Through these considerations you are now ready to put the information covered in this chapter into practice as you build you own unique financial plan.

PART THREE

E – ESTABLISH YOUR PLAN

In this section we will consider budgeting and why it is important to have an understanding of the cost of your lifestyle, however much surplus income you have at this stage. We will also cover insurance and how you can make certain that your loved ones are protected from the financial impact of illness or death, ensuring that your plan can remain on track even if the unexpected occurs.

We look in some detail at investments, both different asset classes and their strengths and weaknesses, as well as different approaches to investment management. We explore how asset classes can be combined to build a diversified investment portfolio and the advantages to different investment approaches.

With this increased understanding you may feel confident to make your own investment decisions and start to build your assets in a more structured manner. You may also have decided that you would rather delegate investment management to a third party. If this is the case, you will have a greater understanding of different investment approaches and be able to seek a professional that works in the way that matches your own preferences.

With this knowledge you will be able to build your first financial plan. While this first draft may have a high level of detail and take you longer than future versions, it is unlikely to be the most accurate, as it will be honed and improved over time as the future starts to become clearer.

7
Budgeting And Saving

To be able to plan for the future, it is important to have an idea of what the cost of your lifestyle is. In my experience, this is something very few people know, so one of the first steps you need to take is to try to understand your expenditure and the things you spend your money on.

Budgeting

These days, thankfully, open banking makes it possible to get a breakdown of expenditure, split into various categories, from many banks. Generally, the categorisation is not perfect, but with a little adjustment you should fairly quickly be able to get an accurate breakdown. I would suggest going back over the past year to ensure you capture any annual costs as well as monthly expenditure and one-off costs. You need to make sure you do the same for any credit cards, and if you run joint finances, you should look across all accounts for you both.

The purpose of this exercise is not to pass judgement on expenditure patterns or to state that you won't spend that much again in the future. In particular, it would be unhelpful to make any comment about a spouse or partner's expenditure at this stage!

Once you have a full year of data, try to break it down into some categories that work for you. I tend to use the following, with some examples given here for each category:

- **Household expenses** – utilities, council tax, food shopping, buildings and content insurance
- **Personal expenses** – clothes, hair care, makeup, gym membership
- **Education** – school fees, personal development costs
- **Children costs** – clothes, pocket money, trips
- **Motoring expenses** – car purchase costs (however funded), petrol, servicing, road tax, insurance
- **Work-related expenses** – travel, coffee and lunch costs at work, work clothes

- **Leisure and entertainment** – restaurants, cinema, golf or tennis club membership
- **Holidays** – all non-business trips, including short breaks and family holidays
- **Property maintenance** – repairs and renewals, pool maintenance
- **Financial** – insurance (life and any others), pension, savings, investments
- **Taxation** – income tax, capital gains tax (council tax is included in household expenses); if your firm holds back a tax reserve, this category may be required only for capital gains

The purpose of categorising is that it allows you to consider how these costs might change over time. For example, school fees will eventually come to an end; holiday costs may change in the future; and if you were to buy a larger or smaller house, household expenses would be adjusted.

As you go through the figures, you will see that some expenses are one-off costs. The first step you need to take when considering these costs is to establish whether they are truly one-off costs. For example, while replacing a boiler may not be something you need to do every year, there should always be something in the budget for property maintenance. Likewise, with holidays this should be a figure that represents what you would normally spend each year. If the year of calculation includes a particularly expensive holiday, you may decide that would not be repeated each year, so this recurring cost can be reduced slightly. It might, though, be worth budgeting more than your average, to allow for more expensive trips every few years; and if you had relatively few trips last year, perhaps that the budget needs to be higher.

As you extract your expenditure from your bank statements, you should also be able to gather information on your income during the same period. This would generally be net of tax, as most (but not all) law firms will retain the tax reserve before providing you with drawings and distributions. The same is also true for employees, as income tax and National Insurance are deducted at source. You then need to add any other sources of income such as rental income, child maintenance or benefit, dividend income and any other income or capital sums you have received in the year. Again, you would need to look out for one-off payments and consider whether they will ever be repeated.

Hopefully, when you compare your income with your expenditure, you will see a surplus. You then need to consider whether the surplus you have identified matches up to an increase in your bank balance over time. If it doesn't, you may have underestimated your expenditure or assumed things are one-offs, when they actually show up in one form or another every year.

What happens, though, if you are spending more than you earn? Even though you may have expected this outcome after seeing your bank balance reduce, the exercise has still been useful. Not only do you now know you are overspending and by how much, but confronting the problem is also good. You now have to carefully consider whether there are any costs that could be reduced. In the first instance identify costs that could be removed without impacting your lifestyle. Rather than trying to find big, painful changes, look for a few small changes that will make a marked difference overall.

While the ideal solution comes from making small changes that have no real impact on your lifestyle, larger adjustments will in some cases be required. For example, rather than three family holidays per year, you might consider adjusting to two; or instead of spending £100,000 per year on home improvements, you could do things more slowly and spend £50,000.

The purpose in all areas is not to do without entirely and not to cut down so much that you feel you are depriving yourself of all pleasures. Too much cost-cutting is sustainable over only a relatively short period of time, and it is normally followed by a blowout in which you snap and complete an extravagant purchase, sometime resulting in you spending more than would have been the case without the reductions.

I have covered a lot of what to do if you are spending more than you should and therefore need to increase your rate of saving, but many of my clients save far more than they need to. If this applies to you – if the saving comes after you spend all you want to and you have a full and rewarding lifestyle – then this is great. It normally indicates that your professional success has resulted in a much higher income than is required for your chosen lifestyle, which is going to help to provide you with significant flexibility over the work you undertake in the future.

For some people, however, the lack of spending has little to do with having a huge surplus and more to do with a fear of running out of money and a feeling that they need to focus solely on the future, at the expense of the present. We will cover this and other difficulties people have with money more in Chapter 12.

To be able to achieve financial freedom and to have the choice whether or not to work requires you to build a plan to get to the number you need. Understanding your current surplus or deficit will make it easier to plan for where you want to get to.

DAVE SAVES

Dave had a problem. Whatever he did, money seemed to slip through his fingers. After two quick promotions at work, he was now earning nearly double what he earned two years earlier, but still, he was running into his overdraft at the end of every month. Yes, he had bought a nicer car, and the monthly payments were £200 higher than he'd been paying before, but that didn't account for where the rest of the extra was going.

I asked Dave to complete a spending log over a two-month period, in which he wrote down exactly what he spent every day. This is not an approach I use often, as quite frankly, recording every penny you spend is not a fun task, and I certainly don't think anybody should live that way. In Dave's case, though, I knew we needed to drill down to work out the reasons for his shortfall.

At the end of the period, we reviewed the details and it was clear Dave was spending a significant amount – around £1,200 per month – on 'stuff' that added nothing to his life. This included an expensive membership to a gym he never went to, multiple trips per day to expensive coffee shops, Uber and taxi rides, and buying clothes that included some he hadn't ever worn.

When we looked through the details, Dave was shocked at what he was spending his money on and stated that it had no impact on his quality of life. We first agreed that, over the next month, he would make a concerted effort to go more regularly to the gym to get some value from it. We then decided on a weekly budget of £100 for spending on extra 'stuff'. If he could stick to this, it would provide a spare £500 per month, which at the end of the month he would move into a savings account. I suggested that he physically withdrew the £100 at the start of the week and spent cash, to make it easier to monitor spending while also making it feel more like he was spending actual money.

We ran this experiment for two months and got together after this period. The change in Dave was astonishing. Not only had he accumulated £1,200 in his savings account during this period – £200 more than we had targeted – but he also had a much better idea of what he was spending his money on, and he was making smarter money choices. He had enjoyed getting back to the gym but found that the facilities at the low-cost gym down the road were just as good, so he had switched and saved around £80 per month in doing so.

He also joined the loyalty scheme of his favourite coffee shop, and while cutting down on trips, he was able to enjoy free coffee every couple of weeks. In six of the nine weeks he had been left with some money from his weekly budget, and although he had exceeded the budget in three weeks, it had been a conscious decision because he'd wanted to buy something in particular. He now found saving to be rewarding and looked forward to seeing how much he could move across to his savings account at the end of each month.

Over the next twelve months Dave was able to put aside £7,500 in his savings account. He then received a promotion and a salary increase of £500 per month, which he decided to use to increase his pension contributions each month, stating, 'I've not had this money, so I won't miss it.'

Dave now regularly saves a good amount each month, while still enjoying doing the things he has always done.

Summary: Budgeting and saving

In this chapter we looked at how to categorise your spending to ensure that you have an understanding of the cost of your lifestyle. This broad information is vital when planning for your financial future. We considered:

- How to use your bank statements to help you to prepare analysis of your spending
- Why it is important to understand your surplus income
- What to do if you are spending more than you earn
- Why spending less is not always the answer

Using budgeting regularly, not to pass judgement on your spending but to understand it, is important while you continue to earn and beyond your working life. It is also likely to reduce your financial anxiety and flag up potential challenges early, allowing more choice around the compromises you make.

8
Protecting What Matters Most

Before you can build your financial plan, you need to ensure that your loved ones are protected if anything happens to you. In this chapter we will consider the different options for insurance to protect your family if you were to die, or if you suffered an illness that prevented you from working. While I have addressed your requirements for protection, this could equally apply to your partner, and it is important to consider the financial implications of death or serious illness for either of you.

Protecting your loved ones

If you are a barrister, this is all down to you, whereas associates will probably have cover provided through the firm, and most of the larger law firms have a policy covering the partners. The first step may therefore be to speak to your firm to see what cover is provided, if any. From the work we did in Part Two, you will have details of your existing cover.

Insurance types

Generally, life insurance becomes more expensive as you age, and some older critical illness policies provide better levels of cover than newer ones, as advances in medical care have resulted in better recovery rates from serious illnesses and therefore a higher threshold being applied before a payout is provided. As a general rule, if the life insurance policy has been in place for more than five years, it is unlikely to be possible to arrange the same cover for a lower cost, because you are five years older and the risk for the insurance company has increased.

After finding out what is provided by your firm, you need to consider how much cover is required. You should start by looking at your mortgage and any other debts and ensuring that these can be paid off if anything happens to you. Ideally, this would be the case in the event of either death or serious illness; if you are experiencing a health crisis, you don't want to have to worry about whether you can afford to keep a roof over your head.

Once you have made sure that any debts and commitments are covered, it is time to turn to family and dependants. With children, consider the costs of school fees; university costs; and costs for clothes, activities and any other child-related costs. Work this out over one year, and then multiply the figure by the number of years until they will finish university, say to the age of twenty-one, or longer if they are likely to study a subject such as medicine. Multiply this by the number of children you have, and you will have a number for the lump sum of cover required.

Moving on to your spouse or partner, assuming that the mortgage is paid off, what level of income would they require? If they have their own career, is this something they would be able to continue at the same level if something happened to you? If not, a provision needs to be made for their living expenses as well as your own if you suffered a serious illness and were unable to work. You can then use the method above to calculate the lump sum level of cover required. If your partner received their pension provisions as well as whatever you have already saved, would that be enough for retirement? If so, you need only to work out shortfalls and have cover running until retirement, with perhaps a shorter period for the provision for children. If there would be a shortfall in retirement, you may need to consider an increase to the amount of cover needed.

Using some of the products explained in Chapter 5, 'Understanding Financial Products And Investments', you can use a range of products to build up the cover you need. To ensure that the mortgage and any other loans are paid off, you could use a term assurance policy with critical illness cover.

For the children you could also use a term assurance policy for the amount that you calculated as a lump sum. Again, it would make sense to include critical illness cover, if possible, so that the policy will pay out if you suffer a serious illness as well as on death. Alternatively, you could arrange a family income benefit policy, which pays out a tax-free amount each month to cover school or university fees. To make sure that you can maintain a comfortable lifestyle if you become unwell, you could take out an income protection policy, which will pay you if you are unable to work for any reason. In addition, a term assurance or further family income benefit for any additional support required by your partner in the event of your death could be arranged.

Although there may be cover that is provided by your firm, you need to take care with this. In a scenario in which you left the firm, the policy would cease, which could leave you without the insurance you need. If you had previously suffered an illness, you could find it very expensive or impossible to arrange replacement cover at that point. Although some policies have an option for you to continue with the plan after leaving the firm, these are quite rare.

Some people take the view that they will entirely disregard any life cover provided through the firm, and this is certainly a sensible approach. For some, because the cost of life insurance can be expensive, a more pragmatic approach is required, but relying solely on cover through the firm may be unwise.

SUSIE AND AISHA – PROTECTION EXAMPLE

Susie is concerned about what would happen if she became sick or died. After the birth of the twins six years ago, Susie's partner Aisha has taken a break from her career in the civil service to look after the children but plans to return to work this year. Susie and Aisha have an outstanding mortgage of £500,000, which is on a repayment basis. The twins go to the local prep school and will go on to the attached day school thereafter.

Although Susie's firm provide £500,000 of life cover through the partnership, Susie has decided to disregard this, as a former partner at the firm became ill and decided to retire from the firm due to ill health. When he died a couple of months later, his family didn't receive the life insurance payout because this had stopped when he left the firm.

Susie and Aisha decide to take out a life and critical illness policy on a decreasing term basis, which is designed to pay off the mortgage should either of them die or suffer a serious illness during the mortgage term. In addition, Susie takes out a family income benefit policy, also with critical illness cover, to cover the cost of school and university fees for the twins until they reach the age of twenty-one. The cover increases at a rate of 5% per annum to allow for the expectation that school fees will rise quicker than general inflation. Although the fees at the prep school are slightly lower than those of the senior school, Susie will base the cover on senior school fees so that Aisha would have a little more for additional childcare, so that she could continue her career. Although they have discussed whether Aisha would require additional income to support her in bringing up the twins alone, they have agreed that Aisha's salary should be sufficient if school fees and the mortgage are taken care of.

Susie also decides to take out an income protection policy, with a deferment period of three months to coincide with the sick pay provisions at her firm. The policy will provide Susie with 50% of her current drawings in the event that she is unable to work as a solicitor for any reason. The cover will continue until she reaches the age of sixty-eight, at which point her state pension and personal pensions or savings could be used to support her lifestyle in retirement. Although Susie and Aisha considered taking out some additional cover for Aisha, they felt that Susie's income would be sufficient to pay for additional childcare if it was required, and with the mortgage paid off from the joint policy, Susie would have sufficient surplus income should Aisha become ill or die.

While putting these policies in place resulted in an increased budget for insurance, Susie and Aisha feel comfortable that, should the worst happen, their family will be looked after, and the survivor will be able to bring up the twins without having to worry too much about money.

Summary: Protecting what matters most

In this chapter we looked at how you ensure that your financial plan will not fail if you or your partner suffers a serious illness or dies. We considered:

- How much insurance you need to protect your family
- How to ensure that your children's education will not be disrupted if something happens to you
- Why relying on life insurance may not be the best approach

Protecting your financial future is generally inexpensive, and it is vital your planning is robust so you are covered if anything happens to your health in the future. Although it may prove unnecessary, if it is required, this planning will make a huge difference.

9
Insight Into Investments

Having worked out what you want to achieve, the surplus funds you have available to allocate to your goals and the products that will be used, it is now time to turn our attention to investments.

Asset classes

There are a range of different asset classes that can be used, and blending them together can help to maximise returns while controlling investment risk. The level of investment risk you are comfortable with does in some ways dictate what the spread of investments should look like.

Looking at the different asset classes that could be used, let's first consider the traditional asset classes.

Cash

As a general rule, you should keep at last six months' expenditure in short-term cash to cover any unexpected occurrences. In most cases convenience is more important than maximising interest for these funds. You may want to hold more cash, perhaps in longer-term saving products for the security and protection of nominal value that they provide. As a general rule, cash is great when capital is required in the short term (up to five years). Over the longer term, investments will generally provide greater returns on average, although this will be accompanied by periods in which investment values fall.

Fixed interest

With a fixed-interest investment, you are investing in the debt of a country or company. Investment returns are provided through regular income payments and, at the end of the term, the repayment of the capital.

Although most corporate debt is arranged with a fixed rate of interest, some index-linked debt is available, in which the interest payments and capital are linked to the rate of inflation.

Government debt and corporate debt, while both fixed interest, tend to be viewed slightly differently. In some cases investors will invest separately in each area, although there are investment funds that have the ability to hold both government and corporate debt within the same fund.

Government debt

UK Government debt is known as gilts, so called because the certificates that used to be issued had a gilded (golden) edge to them. These days they are all held electronically, so if you buy gilts, don't expect a gilded certificate! Gilts are considered to be a risk-free asset because the UK Government has never failed to repay its debts, although that of course doesn't mean it couldn't happen in the future. Gilt rates are used when assessing a risk-free rate of return, which is sometimes used in a model called CAPM (capital asset pricing model), which seeks to determine the expected returns from various investments.

Conventional gilts (as opposed to index-linked gilts) are issued by the Debt Management Office with a fixed term and a fixed interest rate (with fixed-interest payments, known as coupons, paid out twice a year). The price can vary significantly over time, and they are often bought for much less than the £100 par value, particularly if they have a few years to run and the coupon is less than the Bank of England base rate. At maturity you will get back £100 for each unit held.

The value of gilts moves depending on expectations for future interest rates (and changes in interest rates) as well as on sentiment about the economy, domestic and global politics, and other factors.

Because the rate of interest is fixed, when there are movements in the value of gilts, it is the price that changes. When interest rates rise, the yield that investors demand to hold the debt increases and, because the interest rate is fixed, it is the price that has to drop to allow the yield to increase. When interest rates go down, the yield reduces, and the price increases to allow this to happen.

When you purchase gilts, you know what the yield will be if you hold the investment to maturity because you know the price that you paid, the coupons that will be paid out during the term and the redemption price (which is always £100). This therefore provides certainty, although because you don't have to hold to redemption, you can sell at any time.

Gilts are issued with a high coupon (rate of interest) or with a low coupon. Pension funds and those seeking high levels of income tend to favour high coupon holdings as they provide higher cash flows, which can be matched to liabilities. Investors that are holding gilts directly tend to favour low coupon debt, particularly those closer to maturity. This is for tax reasons – you pay income tax at your highest tax rate on interest, including the coupon from gilts. If you buy a low coupon gilt, although the yield will be similar, the coupon is small and most of your return will come through capital growth (as the price is likely to be substantially below the £100 that will be paid on maturity). As we have covered earlier, most investments are subject to capital gains tax on the difference between the cost and sale price, but this is not the case with gilts, and there is no tax on capital gains. Holding gilts can therefore be a good way to invest in a low-risk asset class to generate returns that could exceed those from cash. If the gilts are held to maturity, you have certainty of return; however, as no protection against inflation is included, they cannot be classified as risk-free.

It is possible to purchase index-linked gilts, which generally work in the same way. Because both the income and the capital are linked to inflation and future inflation is unknown, though, it is less easy to predict the return you will achieve. For a number of years index-linked gilts have provided returns that are less than the actual rate of inflation, although in periods of high inflation, this may still be an attractive return.

Corporate bonds

Companies raise finance in much the same way as governments, through the issuing of debt. Most of this is on a fixed rather than index-linked basis, although there are some index-linked corporate bonds in issue. The mechanics of a corporate bond are very similar to those of a gilt, but the added factor is credit risk, in the same way that, if you have a poor credit rating, your bank will charge you more interest for your mortgage. The same is true for companies: those with a strong balance sheet and good profitability will be able to borrow more cheaply than companies that have weaker financial figures as the risk of default is reduced. There are credit rating agencies such as Standard & Poor's and Moody's who provide ratings on corporate debt, and this is a big factor in the yield of these bonds once they trade on the open market. The coupon and the yield are not the same thing, and it is the price divided by the coupon which determines the yield.

Corporate debt with a credit rating of BBB or above is deemed to be investment grade and would typically have a yield that is slightly more than that of gilts. The higher the credit rating, the closer to gilts you would expect yields to be, although you would always expect there to be a difference, which is known as a spread. Corporate debt with a credit rating of less than BBB is known as *high yield bonds* or *junk bonds*. While the latter of these terms perhaps gives an impression that they are not worth holding, lower credit-rated bonds tend to offer higher yields and can therefore be attractive, although they would be considered higher risk as the threat of default is increased.

Although it is possible to buy individual gilts, and many private investors and advised clients do so, buying individual corporate bonds is less common amongst private investors as deal sizes (the amount you have to buy) can be high, and it can be difficult to gain wide diversification. Some money managers will buy individual corporate bonds for their clients, but most investors access corporate bonds through investment funds (as would many gilt investors). There are different types of corporate bond funds available – some that invest only in investment-grade corporate debt, some that hold only high yield. Others hold strategic bond funds, which can be invested across all types of fixed interest, with the investment manager selecting the portfolio they feel will provide the best balance between risk and reward.

Commercial property

Commercial property can provide diversification within an investment portfolio for several reasons:

- Investment returns are provided both from the rental income generated from the properties and from the growth in the value of the property.
- The income stream tends to be predictable as leases are generally long term and relatively secure.
- Most leases include rent reviews, which ensure an element of inflation protection.
- Property values are not directly linked to the stock market.

Although purchasing an individual commercial property would be out of the reach of most individuals (and would lack diversification within the asset class), there are a range of commercial property funds that provide access to this share class.

Property is illiquid, though, and the transaction costs of buying and selling property are high. It also takes a long time to sell or buy a property, which presents a problem for open-ended funds, such as Unit Trusts or OEICs (open-ended investment companies), that invest in commercial property. To balance the access requirements of investors within a daily traded open investment fund with the inherent illiquidity of commercial property, investment funds can impose delays of up to six months on redemptions from these types of funds in periods in which there are significant withdrawals. To protect remaining investors, they can also move the unit price so that sellers of the fund are responsible for more of the transaction costs. Neither of these options is particularly popular with investors, who understandably want to be able to get their money out when they need it and don't want to see a fall in value when they do so.

The alternative is to use an investment trust, which is a closed-ended company with a limited number of shares. With property investment trusts you can always access your money, as your shares can be sold at any time. The price you get for those shares, however, will be whatever somebody is willing to pay, and in periods in which commercial property is unpopular, the price could be much less than the underlying value of the assets held by the trust. As investment trusts are themselves listed on the stock market, the price of a property investment trust will fluctuate daily along with market movement, which can reduce some of the diversification benefits of the asset class.

While commercial property investment has been a staple of investment portfolios for many years, we are seeing more and more private and professional investors decide to no longer have any exposure to this asset class.

Equities

An investment into equities is an investment in the shares of a company, with investment returns provided by a share of the profits of the company – a dividend – and an increase in the value of the company over time, or a combination of the two. When we talk about investing in equities, this normally refers to public limited companies listed on a recognised stock exchange. While it is possible to select individual companies to invest in, for many investors the use of funds grants access to a wide spread of investments and allows diversification between companies.

Over the long term, equities have tended to outperform other asset classes, as companies generally grow more quickly than the economy grows. This growth is not linear, however, and share prices fluctuate significantly over time. This happens all through every day but also over the longer term, with markets moving in cycles. Markets can go up or down on any given day, and we do see sustained periods of either increases or falls in stock markets.

Over the short term it is difficult to predict with any confidence whether markets will go up or down. Looking at the US market, for example, between 1928 and 2025, we see that annual returns over the calendar year have been positive seventy-five times and negative twenty three times.[4] When these negative times will occur is impossible to predict and there is no guarantee in the future that the proportion of positive years will be similar to the past, but it does indicate that equities have the potential to provide strong long-term returns, as has been the case in the past.

Some companies generate high levels of profit that they distribute as dividends, which can either be paid out to provide you with income or reinvested to provide additional returns. Some companies provide few or no dividends, which can be because the company doesn't make a profit, but it could also be that they

4 Figures provided by Dimensional in a private communication to the author.

reinvest most of their profits to provide additional growth. Both approaches are valid. There are examples of companies that are very successful in generating dividends; and of those that have provided strong, long-term returns, despite generating little dividend income. Taxation can be a factor in determining what type of companies should be held, as the tax treatment of dividends and capital growth is different.

As there are stock markets around the world, you can invest in domestic companies or overseas companies or a combination of both.

Traditionally, investors have had a home bias, meaning proportionately more exposure, in our case to UK companies. The advantage of this is that the names can be more familiar, the performance may be more in line with the UK economy, and there is no currency risk (as these companies are priced in sterling).

These days, as international trade has become the norm and most of the constituents of the FTSE 100 are global brands who generate much of their revenue overseas, the rationale for a domestic bias is perhaps less pronounced. Generally, developed markets (UK, Europe, Japan and US) are considered to be more stable than developing markets (China, Far East and South America). Developing markets may provide higher returns, but they are expected to be more volatile as the relevant regulation and laws are less well developed. For most individuals a balance between developed and emerging markets makes sense, with more exposure to developed than emerging markets included within a portfolio.

As with corporate bonds and commercial property, while it is possible to buy individual shares, and many investors do that, for some the use of funds makes sense. This is because a fund provides exposure to a wide range of companies and therefore reduces the risk associated with investing in a single company. This does mean that you may not be exposed to all of the upside that can also be generated by an individual company, but in most cases, following tips or buying companies in expectation that they will show exponential growth can be a high-risk approach. Professional money managers who have a strong track record of finding well-performing companies tend to do so through detailed research – something that it can be difficult for a private investor to allocate the requisite time to. However, if this is something you enjoy, you could set up a small dealing account and allocate small sums to these types of holdings. For every winner, there are countless losers, and while picking the winners before they make it big is difficult, it can be fun trying. Make sure, though, that you speak to your compliance department before buying individual shares, as there will normally be a restriction on buying shares in companies for which the firm is acting, to avoid any possibility of insider trading. Many firms require pre-approval for any individual share purchases.

For most individuals who want to secure their financial future but don't have the time or interest to study financial markets, the use of investment funds provides a good way to access a diversified portfolio of companies, and these funds should over time provide stronger returns than other asset classes. All portfolios should have some exposure to equities, but how much depends on your investment horizon, ie on when the funds will be required and on your risk tolerance. If you will need all of the funds within the next couple of years, equities will not be the best option, as over the short term there is a relatively high chance that you would get back less than you invested. Also, if you worry about your investments and would be concerned if the value fell, even if you didn't need the money for many years, then having less exposure to equities might be better for you; stressing and worrying about your long-term investments is not an enjoyable way to live.

Asset mix

Now that I have run through the main asset classes, you need to consider what proportion of your investments should be held in each. How I arrange this for my clients will differ slightly from how you might do it yourself. I ask my clients to complete a risk questionnaire, which seeks to understand both their tolerance for risk and their ability to withstand losses. We factor that into their long-term objectives and capital availability to determine an appropriate level of risk, and we then keep this under review and make adjustments over time due to changes in their situation, risk requirement or investment experience.

Before considering investment, you need to maintain your emergency fund so that you are able to deal with any short-term or unexpected costs. This could include having to pay for the replacement of home appliances or unexpected medical expenses.

An old rule of thumb, which is used less these days but continues to have some relevance, is that you should have 1% of non-equity investments for every year of your age. A thirty-year-old, for example, would have 70% exposure to equities and 30% in non-equities, while for a sixty-year-old the split would be 40% equities and 60% non-equities. This approach ensures that you reduce equity exposure as you get older and are more likely to require access to the capital. While this approach works quite well for younger ages, for many people in their fifties or sixties it could provide too low an equity exposure, particularly as for many people these years are the prime time to save for retirement. One reason for this is that in many cases the cost of school fees, which has previously taken up a significant proportion of surplus income, has come to an end. Another is that, as we approach our fifties and sixties, retirement or a future after work starts to feel more immediate, and we are therefore more motivated to save more for it.

A traditional, balanced approach would normally consist of 60% equities and 40% non-equities, and that would be a good starting point for most people. You then also need to factor in your own attitude to investment risk. What I really mean here is how you feel when the time inevitably comes that your investments go down rather than up in value. If you are able to be pragmatic about this and see it as a normal part of investing (which it is) and patiently wait for things to recover – perhaps even considering buying more during the dips – you may have an ability to take on slightly more risk. If, however, a fall in the value of your holdings leaves you feeling shocked and upset and keeps coming to mind throughout your working day, then perhaps less risk would be better.

There is no right or wrong approach, and we are all different, but it is important to understand how you react to market falls. You may prefer to have less risk exposure initially, perhaps sticking with the 60/40 approach. One area where I would deviate slightly, if you are under forty-five, is your pension. You will not be able to access the funds for at least thirteen years and may well leave them fully invested for longer. Any short-term volatility is therefore unlikely to have an impact on your long-term savings, so you can afford to take more risk and should consider a higher equity content, provided that you are comfortable with this approach.

The second factor to consider when putting together your asset mix is your time horizon. As stated previously, if you are investing for one or two years, the risk level should ideally be zero, as you don't have enough time to recover from a market fall. Over recent years we have seen many default pension options include something called *lifestyling*, in which the pension is initially invested with a high equity content, which reduces as you get closer to retirement. Initially, this moved almost all of the pension fund to cash and gilts by retirement date, in anticipation of the purchase of an annuity. Having security of capital at retirement is important if you plan to purchase an annuity, as the purchase price of the annuity will have a direct impact on the income you receive for the rest of your life. Having all of your pension fund turned to cash and gilts is less helpful if you plan to access retirement benefits through the use of an income drawdown arrangement, in which the pension remains invested and you draw funds directly from the pension fund each year. This change is reflected in some of the lifestyling options that are available.

Considering the investment horizon is important, and as you get closer to the point at which you will use the money, it makes sense to start to consider reducing the risk to which your investments are exposed.

Whether you select equity and non-equity funds yourself or use a multi-asset fund that makes those decisions for you, it is important to understand the level of risk you are happy to accept, as this will define both the returns you receive and the experience you have, both of which are important to your success.

Summary: Insight into investments

In this chapter we looked at investments in greater detail and considered how you might build your assets over time. We covered:

- The different asset classes that can be used to build an investment portfolio
- The various pros and cons of each individual asset class
- How to blend asset classes together to diversify your portfolio
- Why diversification reduces investment risk
- The impact that time horizons have on the level of investment risk you take

By understanding investments, you can ensure that your capital is working hard for you, which can take years off the journey to financial freedom, compared with holding only cash.

10
Building Your Financial Roadmap

You now have all you need to build your financial plan. You have your vision for the future, both short and long term; you have analysed your existing holdings; you have calculated your budget and know what your surplus income is. You have also considered the protection of your family and made the necessary provisions in this area. You are now ready to start pulling everything together into the long-term plan.

Building the financial plan

While I use financial planning software, which provides a full analysis of lifetime cash flow, a relatively simple spreadsheet for this purpose is sufficient for this part of the process. You can download a template at www.financialfreedomforlawyers.co.uk or by scanning the QR code below, but you can construct your own if you prefer.

Your plan needs to include years (or ages) over the period for which you want to run your analysis. I would suggest including a period beyond what would be considered to be normal life expectancy, so perhaps running to 90, 95 or 100; I use 100 in my planning work. The purpose of this is to ensure that you don't run out of money while you are still alive, accepting also that this might mean you don't get to use it all during your lifetime.

You should include sections for investments and pensions, with columns for both investment and withdrawals as well as running totals of values. You can then plug in what you plan to invest, from the surplus you have available until the time you plan to stop working. At that point you move to the withdrawal stage and start to take from the portfolio the money you need to support your lifestyle.

With both contributions and withdrawals you need to make some allowance for inflation, so select a level of inflation that you would expect to apply as a first step.

You can then either apply that inflation rate to both your contributions and your withdrawals, ensuring you inflation-adjust your withdrawals to reflect the level of inflation you have selected.

Alternatively, you can view your contributions and withdrawals as being in real terms, ie the current purchasing power of those values. In this scenario you can leave values the same, but you need to adjust investment returns for inflation. For example, if you plan to use an assumption that investment returns will be 6% per annum on average and inflation will be 2% per annum on average, you will use a net return of 4%.

While this second approach makes it easier to understand the figures you are looking at, you need to make sure you increase your investments by inflation each year. For example, if you have assumed within your schedule £50,000 per distribution investments each year and allowed for a 5% increase each year as you become more senior and move up the points scale (or whatever method of increased income you have), you need to also allow for inflation within this increase; if this was 3%, you would therefore increase your £50,000 investment by 8% (5% + 3%) to £54,000.

Either approach works. Just make sure that you pick the one you are comfortable with and truly understand, because finding a mistake in your calculations once you have stopped working could have a significant impact on your retirement lifestyle.

Before considering any investments, however, you should repay any credit card or high-interest debt that you hold. This is because the interest is likely to be higher than any investment return you generate, so it's better to pay off the interest immediately rather than invest the money, taking investment risk, when repaying the debt is risk-free.

With your surplus income, make sure you first fund tax-efficient holdings. In the first instance, make use of your pension and ISA allowances. If you are saving as a couple, consider using both of your allowances. These allowances would give a minimum of £53,600 of available investments for a couple. This is assuming one has high enough income to have a reduced or tapered pension allowance (£10,000); and the other doesn't work and is therefore restricted to a pension contribution of £3,600. In reality, though, most people would be able to save more than this in a tax-efficient environment.

Taking up some or all of your tax-efficient savings may be the extent of what you are able to do. If this is sufficient to allow you to achieve your long-term goals, then this is perfect and you can stop here. The only other thing to consider is whether you fund a pension or an ISA or a combination of both. The pension provides tax relief on contributions as well as tax-free growth and 25% as a tax-free lump sum (subject to limits) and so is a very tax-efficient way to save. The ISA does not benefit from tax relief but grows tax-free and can provide tax-free capital and

PART FOUR
A - ACT ON IT

In this section of the book we look at the implementation of your financial plan. We will cover how you will know when you reach your goals and consider different approaches to life after law.

We will also consider some of the areas that can hold you back from achieving your goals and some strategies to overcome them. This is a long-term process, and there will inevitably be setbacks and things that don't entirely go to plan. There may even be situations that force you to re-evaluate everything you have done so far. The discipline you have shown and the progress you will make over time, though, will mean you have the resources and resilience to be able to handle these adjustments.

11
Finding Your Financial Confidence

What is my number? How much do I need to save to have a comfortable life without ever having to worry about running out of money? I have seen some financial planners use these questions as marketing tools, and I understand it. It is comforting to think that it can all be boiled down to a single number, a sort of meaning of life, the universe and everything, although I doubt £42 will get you far.

Sadly, I don't think planning fits quite as neatly into place as this. In this chapter, though, we can consider some general principles that will guide us towards knowing when we have enough.

How much is enough?

The first element is to understand the cost of our lifestyle. This is an important consideration because many of us have no idea of how much our lifestyle costs.

What does your lifestyle cost?

If you have worked through this book from the start, you will have already carried out much of this work, although depending on your resources, you may not have needed to look too closely at spending. At this stage it is vital to have a good idea of what your lifestyle costs, as once you 'pull the parachute' on retirement, you really don't want to be forced to go back to work.

Make sure that in this element you factor in any additional costs that will apply post-retirement, as having more time on your hands will normally mean you spend more (which is the opposite of how most retirement plans work), although some debt and work-related costs will be removed.

How much guaranteed income will you receive?

The next step is to consider any guaranteed income. This would generally be state pension but could include any defined benefit pensions you and your partner have accumulated. This guaranteed income should be deducted from the cost of your lifestyle in retirement, to give a shortfall figure. If these sums come into payment after your intended retirement date, we will need to consider an adjustment. For this purpose, work out how many years before receipt of these benefits you will retire, and then multiply the number of years by the amount of income provided to get a capital sum.

Lump sum

With the annual shortfall you have worked out, we need to turn this into a lump sum. While I use a more precise approach with my clients, for the interest of simplicity we are going to work on a factor of 25. Put simply, for every £10,000 of income you require, you will need to save £250,000. This approach uses a sustainable withdrawal rate of around 4% (which can be used in the calculation if you find that easier). This is known as the 4% rule and was calculated by Bill Bengen – an engineer turned financial adviser in the US in the 1990s.[5] He wanted to calculate how much you could withdraw from a portfolio over thirty years without risking running out of money. He looked back at 120 years of US stock market performance and

5 WP Bengen, 'Determining withdrawal rates using historical data', *Journal of Financial Planning* (1994), 14–24; reproduced by the Financial Planning Association (2004), www.financialplanningassociation.org/sites/default/files/2021-04/MAR04%20Determining%20Withdrawal%20Rates%20Using%20Historical%20Data.pdf, accessed 12 March 2026

came up with a figure of 4% of your initial investment pot, increasing with inflation each year, as being a sustainable level of withdrawal.

Although this research provides a nice, neat number that is simple and easy to remember, there are some drawbacks to this simplified approach. It is generally based on a 50% domestic equity and 50% government debt approach, which may not align to your own risk tolerance and preferences. The outcome can vary significantly depending on the sequence of investment returns, with significant falls in markets early in retirement creating a far less comfortable retirement than strong early returns.

Other considerations

Given that outcomes can vary, a more tailored approach to understanding your requirements can be worthwhile. To do this we return to the 'What does your lifestyle cost?' step above and, rather than just defining our retirement costs, we need to break them down into necessary and discretionary expenses. Now that we know how much we must have to live on and how much is nice to have rather than essential, it might make sense to you to ensure you have enough secure income to cover this minimum living standard. Some of this may come from the existing secure income you have (state pension, for example), but you can also purchase guaranteed income through an annuity, which would increase the secured income you receive. The cost of this would depend on a number of factors, including interest rates, gilt yields and life expectancy data, as well as the options you chose to include within the annuity you purchased. Remaining funds can therefore remain invested and be allocated to discretionary spending.

One retirement challenge is the timing of investment withdrawals and the volatility of markets. If you are willing to adjust your discretionary spending depending on market conditions, you can maximise the possibility that your capital will last as long as you do. This may mean having to put off doing things you want to do until market conditions allow for them; or accepting that you take funds from lower-risk assets in periods of equity market falls, to preserve the more volatile assets until the prices recover.

Long-term care

At this stage, you don't know if you will need long-term care, but if you do, the costs could be significant. How will it be funded? If residential care is needed and you own your own home, maybe this cost can be covered; but what if you need a little care and want to remain in your home? How you allow for this in your planning depends on your viewpoint and perhaps your own experience with parents or grandparents.

You can work out an estimated cost and allow for this within your calculations of how much you will need. This approach will ensure you can pay for long-term care if you need it, without being a burden on your family (which is normally an important consideration). There is a risk, though, that this care will not be needed at all, which could have left you working for longer than needed or spending less in active retirement.

While you could ignore long-term care entirely, that would probably not be sensible, as there is a strong possibility for a couple that at least one of you will need some kind of assistance in later life.

Adjustment to lump sum

These considerations take us away from having a nice, neat number to work towards, so can we simplify things again to help us to have something to work towards? Perhaps we could take our £250,000 for every £10,000 of income (or 4%) requirement and then add an additional 'comfort' factor, to allow for the volatility of returns and the prospect of requiring long-term care. Rather than trying to calculate an accurate figure, we can set this factor at between 10% and 25%. Obviously, the bigger the comfort factor, the more you will be able to cope with volatility and the unexpected, but also the more you will need to save and the longer you may need to work. If you are prepared to be flexible in your retirement expenditure, depending on market conditions, and you are happy to accept that you may need to use the value of your house for long-term care, then you can keep your comfort factor low. Conversely, if you would prefer the security of knowing that, whatever happens, everything will be fine; and if you want to go on an expensive trip next year, you jolly well will, regardless of what your portfolio is doing, then a higher comfort factor is required.

Bringing it back to the number

Let's say you have worked out that the amount of income you require in retirement is £100,000 per annum, net of taxation. This will be sufficient to maintain a comfortable lifestyle throughout retirement and ensure that, should you require long-term care in later life, you will be able to fund it. We then need to consider how much, if any, secured income you will receive.

Secured income is income that is guaranteed and will be paid to you regardless of what happens in the future. In many cases this income is index linked and so protected from the impact of inflation. Examples of secured income are state pension, defined benefit pension arrangements (final salary or career average earning arrangements) and annuities that can be bought with pension funds or cash.

Secured income

Let's take an example, where you and your partner will both receive a full state pension of £12,000 each, and one of you has a £10,000 NHS pension, giving total secured income of £34,000 per annum.

The state pension will use your personal allowance, ie the amount you can earn without paying income tax each year, so it will not be subject to taxation. The NHS pension will be taxable. When allowing for taxation, we want to try to keep things simple, and although current tax rates are 20%, 40% and 45%, there are elements that will not be subject to taxation, even within the taxable elements of your capital. For example, the pension commencement lump sum (PCLS) from the pension is tax-free up to a limit, while capital gains are taxed at 18% for basic rate taxpayers and include an exemption. For this reason we are going to use a tax rate of 15% on taxable income.

If your target income is more than £150,000 pa for a couple (or £75,000 for a single individual), this tax rate would need to increase on amounts above these levels to around 40%. You also need to take care if your capital is unevenly split between a couple, as tax rates are calculated individually, so equalising income between you can be helpful in keeping taxation as low as possible. This is not possible with pensions, but investments can be moved freely between married spouses and civil partners, though this doesn't apply to unmarried couples.

Your secured income of £34,000 includes £24,000 of state pension, which uses your personal allowance and is therefore not subject to taxation. The £10,000 of NHS pension is taxable and, allowing for 15% taxation, would provide you with net income of £8,500 (15% of £10,000 is £1,500; £10,000 - £1,500 is £8,500). Your net secured income is therefore £24,000 plus £8,500, ie £32,500 in total.

You plan to stop working at fifty-seven, and this secured income is paid out from your sixty-seventh birthday. You therefore have a shortfall of £32,500 for ten years – £325,000 – in respect of your secure income. At this stage I have ignored both investment returns and inflation, which should balance each other out.

Unsecured income

To make this £32,500 of income up to the £100,000 you require, you will also need £67,500 of unsecured income.

We then need to understand how much of this will come from taxable and non-taxable pension and investments. If we assume 25% is from ISAs, and 75% comes from a combination of pension and taxable investments, we can then apply taxation to our required income.

£16,875 requires no adjustment, as it comes from your ISA holdings.

This leaves £50,625 as required income but this is subject to taxation of 15%. To work out how much gross income you require you would need to use a gross up formula as follows:

$$\text{Gross income} = \frac{\text{Net income}}{1 - \text{Tax rate}}$$

$$\text{Gross income} = \frac{£50{,}625}{1 - 0.15}$$

$$\text{Gross income} = \frac{£50{,}625}{0.85}$$

The gross income required is £59,558.82.

The table below breaks down these calculations.

Income calculation

Source	Amount	Taxation rate	Taxation amount	Net income
State pension	£24,000	0%	£0	£24,000
NHS pension	£10,000	15%	£1,500	£8,500
ISA income	£16,875	0%	£0	£16,875
Investment income	£59,559	15%	£8,934	£50,625
Total income	**£110,434**		**£10,434**	**£100,000**

Capital required

The total unsecured income you need each year is therefore £59,559 plus £16,875, a total of £76,434. We then apply our 4% factor (£76,434/4%) or our £10,000 per £250,000 formula (7.6434 × £250,000) to get £1,910,850.

Adding our ten-year secured income shortfall of £325,000 gives us £2,235,850. We then need to add the comfort factor we have decided to apply. In this example I will use 10%, as the individuals in question are quite happy to reduce their expenditure in periods of poor stock market returns. This gives a comfort factor of £223,585 (10% of £2,235,850. When added to a capital requirement of, £2,235,850 we have a total capital requirement of £2,459,435 which in this case I would round up to £2.5 million.

Capital calculation

Capital type	Amount	Period (years)	Factor	Total
Secured Income shortfall	£32,500	10		£325,000
Unsecured income	£76,434		25	£1,910,850
Subtotal				**£2,235,850**
Comfort factor	£2,235,850		10%	£223,585
Total				£2,459,435

In this example, these individuals will need to save a total of £2.5 million, of which at least £425,000 (16,875 × 25, rounded up) must be ISAs, by the time they reach the age of fifty-seven, for them to be able to stop working and have £100,000 of net income each year.

What does good look like?

At each milestone it is important to consider what the next step looks like and what would represent success. This helps you to celebrate success but also to be honest with yourself, when what may look like good progress on the outside doesn't quite match up to your ambition.

Once you reach a milestone – perhaps paying off your mortgage or reaching a certain level in your investments and pensions – it is important to celebrate and enjoy the fact that you have achieved something important. With investment values, the nature of markets means you might dip below your milestone again through market conditions, but that doesn't matter; it is the initial achievement that is important. These steps are hard to achieve, and they are not something that everybody will be as disciplined as you in achieving.

Setting the next milestone is then important, and it should be challenging but achievable. Ideally, you should be trying to reach milestones every couple of years, so the next one should not be too distant in the future. Each milestone is an opportunity – in addition to during the forward planning reviews – to revisit the long-term vision to understand whether that still represents a version of the future that fills you with excitement and anticipation. This future vision will change as time goes on. For some that change will be minor and represent no more than a development of their thinking. For others the change may be fundamental and can result in something that looks entirely different to your original vision. Neither is wrong or to be feared, and the progress you have made will give you the flexibility to allow for a fundamental change, which wouldn't have been possible without your hard work.

A new client, who was about to retire, once came to me. Although they had made plans, they felt those plans were no longer aligned to what they now wanted. They said, 'I feel like I have spent thirty years climbing a ladder, and I now find out that it is resting against the wrong wall.' While I did manage to steer them to a better 'wall' and achieve a better outcome, the lack of time between planning and execution meant they had to make more compromises than they would have liked.

Make sure you keep a check on the wall your ladder is resting against!

THE REWARDING RETIREMENT – WALKING IN THE SCOTTISH HIGHLANDS

George was coming to the end of a varied and successful career as managing partner at a large firm of corporate lawyers.

He had achieved much in his career and built up substantial assets. As we discussed his retirement aspirations, it became clear that his dream retirement was well thought out and would be rewarding. As he spoke about his plans, I could see a change in his entire demeanour; his body language became more expressive, and he broke into a half smile as he explained what he planned to do.

He intended to move to the Highlands of Scotland to spend his time walking and fishing. He had already purchased a mountain lodge for £150,000 and was expecting to spend £75,000 on renovations, to get the lodge exactly as he wanted it. Having travelled extensively in his younger years, he had no real desire to see the world and would be quite happy simply spending time walking in the hills, fishing in the salmon river next to the lodge and photographing the wildlife and scenery around him.

This was something of a shock to me and also to his existing adviser, who had worked with him for many years, diligently building up a portfolio of pensions and investments of around £10 million. George also owned a London property, valued at around £5 million, which he was planning to sell ahead of his move to Scotland. Although we discussed him retaining a London flat or other properties, this was not something he wanted to do, as he was eager to get away from London.

While it was very straightforward to come up with a plan that would ensure George could enjoy his retirement without running the risk of running out of money – with his modest lifestyle and significant portfolio, he could live to 1,000 and still have plenty of capital – it made me think, *What might have happened if we had this conversation earlier?*

His adviser was highly competent and would, I am sure, have spoken about future aspirations with George. I suspect but don't know for certain that George had been so focused on his work that he hadn't really spent time thinking about it before.

Had he thought about what he wanted to do, he could have retired ten or twenty years earlier. Whether he would have done that is, of course, another question, but that knowledge may have reduced his stress levels, while he was working and, who knows, may have resulted in him stopping at least a few years earlier.

The lesson here is the plan. At the very least you should have one!

Summary: Finding your financial confidence

We have considered how much you need to save to give you the ideal lifestyle after work. Some of the areas covered were:

- How much income is required to maintain your lifestyle once your income stops

- How to turn this into a capital amount
- What allowance should be made for taxation and unexpected situations
- How to maintain your motivation over time in the face of temptation and distractions

You now have a clear idea of the amount of capital that will be required to fund your lifestyle. This gives you both a target and a measure of when you reach financial freedom, at which point the question of whether you continue in the legal profession will be by choice rather than necessity.

help others, have fun, buy love or reach goals? Or what else was it used for?

4. What are the one-sentence messages regarding money that stuck with you from your childhood? Where did you hear these messages?
5. What were the spending patterns of a) your mother and b) your father?
6. Describe the work ethic of your mother and father.
7. When you were young, did you consider your family to be rich or poor? Or how else did you perceive your situation?
8. What were you taught about money when you were growing up?
9. In your family, was money an issue – a source of conflict – or a tool for achieving goals?
10. When did you first start earning your own spending money?
11. What was your first big purchase? How did it make you feel?
12. As an adult, what has been the most important lesson you have learned about money?
13. In your current financial life, are you more of a spender or a saver?
14. In your current financial life, are you more of an avoider or a worrier?

15. In your heart of hearts, what have you wanted money to give you?
16. Has money been an issue or source of conflict in your important relationships?
17. What money habits have brought you closer to your life goals?
18. What money habits have been obstacles to you reaching your life goals?
19. What or who has most influenced your financial philosophy? How and why?
20. What experience do you feel has most directly shaped your current level of financial satisfaction?

What did you learn by answering these questions? Did it provide you with any insight into the source of your attitudes and behaviour around money? Will the exercise change how you think about your financial life in the future?

Handling setbacks

Along your journey to financial freedom, there will inevitably be setbacks and challenges. If defining how you would like your future life to be and then putting everything in place to achieve it was easy, everybody would be doing it, and every older person you met would have a permanent smug grin on their face!

Sadly, this isn't the case, but that doesn't mean it is not possible.

In your profession you have an advantage of being well rewarded for your hard-earned expertise and experience, but the road still might not be easy. Sometimes things will happen that knock you off track. Some of those things will be enforced; for example, distributions might be less than expected, or you may have to move to a new firm. Others will be due to a change in objectives or goals, eg you decide to buy a bigger house, or you change your plans for retirement to something more costly. At these points it is important to reassess and analyse, to make the necessary adjustments to your planning before moving on with the new plan. Sometimes the setbacks will be temporary, for example as a result of an indulgent purchase, and you may feel bad that you have been set back on your plan. It is important, though, to put those thoughts out of your mind and, rather than thinking about what you could have done differently, concentrate on taking the steps you need to keep moving forwards. Giving up, or deciding that planning your ideal future is not right for you and you should just see what happens, is unlikely to provide you with an optimal outcome, so knuckle back down and commit to steps you can achieve.

If you consistently fall off track, then maybe the plan is not right for you. Perhaps you have been too ambitious about what you can achieve and the sacrifices now are too high, or maybe you don't like the future you have mapped out enough to go without things today. Over the years I have seen all of these happen, and at this point it is time to sit down with your partner and have that serious conversation about what you really want for the future. Are these things aligned between you? If not, are there compromises that would work for you both?

Self-sabotage

Self-sabotage can be a factor, and I have seen this come from one partner or both. It takes place when the allure of short-term gratification is too much to resist and resources are directed away from the long-term goal. As covered previously, I prefer an approach that is not so focused on saving as to leave no capacity for enjoyment and discretionary lifestyle expenditure along the way. If you exclusively target the long term, you create an environment in which you are relying on willpower, which is a limited resource, and it is almost inevitable you will eventually snap and get off track again by splashing out. A better approach is to be more balanced in your saving and spending so you can do some of the things that are really important to you immediately while also saving for the future.

Even if you take this approach, though, there will certainly be times you will be tempted to buy or experience things that directly impact on your ability to stick to the plan. This is where holding each other to account or having an accountability partner can be helpful. Their job is not to say you can't do it; you are a grown adult and have earned the right to choose. They just need to question whether this thing – whatever you feel the need to spend money on – is important enough to impact the long-term plan. Once they have raised the question, however, they need to respect your view or opinion, at least with the first setback, especially if it is minor. Obviously, though, if setbacks are consistent and prolonged, more serious questions need to be asked:

- Is the plan actually important to you?
- Does it need to be more modest and less ambitious to allow more to be spent now?
- If so, does that work for the partner as well?

Again, we come back to compromises and adjustments, and it is far better to make these when you have time ahead of you to earn and save than when you feel you can no longer work.

MIKE'S STORY

Mike was 'on top of his game'. He had been a senior partner, in a large regional firm of solicitors, for seven years. Seven years that had seen significant growth in the firm, with earnings per partner growing well above industry average.

Despite this success, though, Mike was feeling unsettled. He was worried about the amount of effort required to achieve these successes and knew that things might quickly slide if he let up. His efforts to build a team to succeed him had yielded mixed results. A couple of his partners had stepped up to the mark, but others were failing to thrive when given additional responsibility.

Most of all, Mike was tired. He was ready to walk away but felt trapped. Trapped by his responsibilities to the firm, but even more so because he didn't feel he could afford to retire; and anyway, *Who retires at fifty-eight these days?*

We spent some time discussing what Mike would do if he stepped down from his role, and he explained that he loved skiing. He mentioned he would like to be able to spend a week or two, a couple of times a year, renting a lodge in the Alps and skiing, either alone or with friends. As a young student, he had enjoyed art, but rather than follow any artistic pursuits, he had been encouraged to focus on more academic subjects. However, he had a yearning to rediscover his creative side. He also wanted somehow to give back to his community by taking on some kind of volunteering role, although he had no idea what.

Understanding Mike's background and what he wanted from life was essential. He had paid off his mortgage and was widowed, with two grown-up children who were financially independent, so he had no significant financial commitments. The activities he wanted to pursue were relatively inexpensive, and when we discussed his lifestyle, it became clear that it was relatively modest, given his income.

We were able to work together to build a plan that showed he could afford to step away from work immediately if he wanted to. Although he had not accrued as much as he felt he should have done during his working life, his existing pensions and investments were sufficient for the retirement lifestyle he wanted.

Mike spent the next twelve months considering all different scenarios and situations we had modelled.

We looked too at what would happen if Mike remarried and if he needed to help his children with a large expense. We considered a severe global recession, or Mike suffering a serious illness and requiring significant care. In any such scenario, we were able to demonstrate that his financial position would be fine, even if he had stopped working. Obviously, some situations looked better than others, and with some of the more pessimistic assumptions, things did look a little dicier than either of us would have liked. Finally, we reached the point at which he was happy to accept that, as he put it, 'My parachute is packed, and I am ready to leap off the cliff.'

It took Mike a further year to prepare his team for his departure, and while that was by no means plain sailing, some of his partners excelled in taking on more responsibility, and the choice of replacement senior partner became clear to all. Mike was able to walk away knowing the firm was in safe hands. He made peace with the notion that different decisions would be made than when he was in charge, and they would either be more or less successful. That was OK. It was time for new ideas.

Mike became the secretary of the regional swimming association that his daughter had been heavily involved with as a child. It brought him into contact with a whole new circle of friends and allowed him to use the skills he had developed in his career in law, without the pressure that went with it. (Although taking on the task of rewriting the association's rule book was perhaps more work than he had anticipated!)

He started to take regular skiing trips, generally one each year with a group and the other alone, although it has become a tradition for his son to join him for at least part of one of the weeks each year (at Mike's expense, of course), which gives Mike more pleasure than he had expected. Having quiet time with Scott takes him back to when the kids were young.

This summer I am looking forward to attending the first exhibition of Mike's art, alongside that of others from his art class. While none of his paintings will win prizes or sell for millions, that is not the point. He is proud of the work he is producing and now enjoys embracing his creative side.

Summary: Overcoming financial anxiety and setbacks

In this chapter we considered the things that will stop you from achieving the financial future you are planning and what you can do to stay on track. We covered:

- The impact our early memories around money have on our financial approach

- How we can change our attitude and beliefs around money
- Understanding setbacks and what to do when they inevitably happen
- Building resilience in our financial planning

It is inevitable there will be setbacks or challenges as you go through the implementation of your financial plan. Some will be forced upon you; others will be of your own making. This is all part of the process and will require you to assess, adjust and refocus to ensure that you achieve a great outcome, even if it looks very different from your original intention.

13 Financial Planning Example

In this chapter I will outline a realistic financial plan for a fictional couple. While their circumstances and preferences may differ in many ways from your own, seeing the background thinking, the planning structure and the way that details are presented will help you when you come to plan your own journey to financial freedom.

Financial considerations

Deepak and Priya have been planning their financial future. They are both forty-one and have two children, Maya (seven) and Aarvind (four). Deepak is a barrister in ABC Chambers, earning £250,000 per annum; Priya works part-time as an accountant in a local practice and earns £30,000. They have a repayment mortgage on their home, with twenty years to run, and a balance of £500,000. The property is valued at £1 million. Their mortgage interest rate is 4% per annum, and for simplicity, we have assumed this will stay constant throughout the mortgage term (although we know this will not be the case).

They have worked out they can save £60,000 a year at the moment. This is likely to increase by around £2,000 each year until they finish paying school fees, which will happen in fourteen years, when Aarvind is eighteen.

Although they expect university costs thereafter, Priya's parents have covered these costs for her brother's children and have suggested they will do the same for Priya's children. Deepak and Priya therefore expect to be able to increase annual savings by around £30,000 once the school fees finish. For simplicity, I have assumed all figures are in real terms and increase in line with inflation.

We will assume investment returns of 3% above inflation per annum from pensions and investments. (If we assumed that inflation was 3% per annum, this would give an investment return of 6% net of all fees, which is a realistic assumption for investment returns.)

Deepak and Priya have focused so far on reducing the mortgage and have allocated relatively little until now to savings, pensions and investments. Deepak has around £100,000 in a personal pension; Priya has £25,000 in an employee-sponsored scheme, to which her employer pays 5% of her salary. They have joint savings of around £60,000, split between current account, savings account and a cash ISA of £20,000 in Priya's name.

Apart from Priya's death in service life insurance scheme, covering three times her salary, they have no other life insurance.

Life planning

When considering the future, Deepak and Priya say they would like to travel extensively in retirement but have no desire to own a property abroad. Although they have spoken about moving home, they love the property they currently have and can see themselves staying in it for the rest of their lives. They both enjoy dancing and plan to do that more in retirement. Priya is also a keen gardener and would like to be able to spend more time working on the garden in the future.

They have worked out they will require around £75,000 per annum to provide them with a comfortable lifestyle in retirement. They would like to have another £35,000 to use for travel in earlier retirement, which could be used for long-term care if needed in later retirement. Although they don't want to work until the state retirement age of sixty-eight, they would be happy to work until sixty-five, as their parents did.

Protection

To ensure that the family would be protected should anything happen to Deepak or Priya, they decide to take out:

- Income protection of £125k pa for Deepak, running until he is sixty-five, costing £70 per month, with premiums and cover increasing by inflation each year
- Family income benefit of £30k pa, increasing at 5% per annum, until Aarvind finishes secondary education (to cover school fees), costing £30 per month, increasing by 5% each year
- £1.5 million life and critical illness cover until the age of sixty, costing £800 per month, with premiums and cover increasing with inflation each year

Although this may not fully protect the family, Deepak and Priya feel comfortable with this level of cover and cost.

This leaves £48,000 available, which they decide to invest in three ways:

- £20,000 every year in an investment ISA
- £6,000 added to Deepak's pension and £2,000 to Priya's pension

- Additional savings allocated each year proportionately to each pension – 75% to Deepak and 25% to Priya – to benefit from higher tax relief from Deepak's pension

As we run this forward, we can observe:

1. As Deepak and Priya will repay their mortgage before they retire, they can save the surplus.
2. As they get closer to retirement, Deepak's pension contributions will exceed the annual allowance and so will be capped. The excess could be allocated to Priya's pension or elsewhere. In this example I have assumed that they take out a GIA for the previous mortgage payments and surplus after Deepak reaches annual allowance.

The table below shows the capital Deepak and Priya will have accumulated by the age of sixty-five. They would like an income of £110,000 each year in total.

Financial investment	Capital
ISA	£1,500,000
Deepak pension	£1,280,000
Priya pension	£525,000
GIA	£145,000
Total	**£3,450,000**

Using the information from Chapter 11, we work out that Deepak and Priya would receive a full state pension, so £12,000 each. They plan to retire at sixty-five rather than sixty-seven, so they will need to use £24,000 (which we will assume comes from the ISA) for the extra two years. This needs to be deducted from the capital sum, leaving £3.426 million. Using our calculation of £10,000 of income requiring £250,000 of capital, or 4%, this equates to £137,000. However, we then need to adjust for taxation and comfort factor.

Looking at taxation first: the pension represents £1,805,000. Our capital calculation gives £72,200, and reducing for 15% taxation gives net income of £61,370. The non-ISA investments of £145,000 provide gross income of £5,800, reduced to £4,930 when allowing for taxation. This gives a total from pension and taxable investments of £66,300.

In addition, the ISAs, which are tax-free, can provide £59,040 of income (£1,476,000 × 4%), giving unsecured income of £125,340 and total income, including state pension of £24,000, of £149,340. We then need to apply the comfort factor to the unsecured income, which Deepak and Priya have decided should be 20%.

This reduces Deepak and Priya's income by £25,068 (£125,340 x 20%) to £100,240. Added to this would be their state pension of £24,000, giving a total income in retirement of £124,272 (which, for ease, I will round down to £124,000).

The table below shows this calculation.

Source	Capital	Income	Taxation rate	Taxation amount	Net income
State pension	£0	£24,000	0%	£0	£24,000
Pension	£1,805,000	£72,200	15%	£10,830	£61,370
Non-ISA investment	£145,000	£5,800	15%	£870	£4,930
ISA	£1,476,000	£59,040	0%	£0	£59,040
Subtotal	**£3,426,000**	**£161,040**		**£11,700**	**£149,340**
Comfort factor 20% of unsecured income					£25,068
Total					**£124,272**

This figure of £124,000 is more than Deepak and Priya's target of £110,000 per annum, meaning they have some headroom. This could be used to provide more security to the plan, which is always a good idea because investment markets are volatile and investment returns may not be as we have assumed.

Alternatively, they could use the headroom to make an adjustment. That adjustment will depend on their personal preferences, but they could decide to save less and therefore spend more on their current lifestyle, or to retire earlier than planned by working out when they will reach their target and stopping then. They can start saving as much as they can and have the confidence that there is some wiggle room within the figures, so if their plans change or something unexpected happens, they can more easily adjust. Your approach to a surplus may be different depending on your views and outlook, but having options is always helpful.

If these figures showed a shortfall, Deepak and Priya may have to make some compromises. This could be the need to find some more savings, either now or in the future. Alternatively, they could work longer or adjust their future lifestyle, although I would suggest caution with this option, as they wouldn't want to have a meticulous plan for a future that is unappealing.

Working towards a future that inspires and excites you will help to keep you on track and, if necessary, to make additional sacrifices to ensure that it happens.

This code provides a link not only to the financial planning spreadsheet for this example but also to templates you can use for your own financial planning. You'll find two versions of this:

1. A template in which you can provide details of the savings you can make
2. A template that allows you to select the income and financial freedom age, and the table will then work out the savings you need to make

You will note from those templates that I have deliberately tried to simplify things. For example, I have assumed that current ISA and pension allowances remain the same over the period, and I have shown figures in today's terms – ie adjusted for inflation. As ISA and pension limits are not index linked, to be accurate I should perhaps reduce them by the rate of inflation each year. However, it is also possible and likely that over a long period these limits will eventually change. I have also assumed relatively simple allowances for future investment returns, based on annual averages. We know investment returns will not be linear, but for the purpose of planning these assumptions are sufficiently accurate to be helpful guides.

Summary: Financial planning example

In this chapter we have looked in detail at an example of a financial plan. We reviewed:

- How to calculate a financial shortfall
- Differentiating between secure and unsecure income

- Allowing for taxation
- Including a comfort factor
- Considering how to approach a projected surplus or deficit

Planning for the future in an uncertain world is difficult. The planning process can also be complex, and it will require regular adjustments and amendments. I hope this example provides a helpful framework that you can use in your own planning.

PART FIVE

M – MONITOR AND MODIFY

The final part of the DREAM approach is to monitor progress and make any adjustments required. When navigating over a long distance, a sailor will initially plot a course but will then make numerous adjustments to that course to allow for weather conditions, obstacles and challenges along the way. Financial planning is similar, although it is not unusual for the final destination to look substantially different from originally envisaged. (I don't think a sailor aiming for New York would be too happy to find themselves coming ashore in Boston!)

Using a four-stage process of Review, Expectations, Analysis and Plan – REAP – you can take the necessary steps to review progress regularly and make the changes required to keep your planning on track, even if events have moved it substantially off course.

The final chapter is designed to help new partners of law firms to navigate those first couple of years. Most of my experience is with international law firms who have UK operations in London, but much is similar within successful law firms all over the UK.

14
Forward Planning

Now that you have your strategy mapped out and have selected your products and investment approach, you need to follow your plan consistently. If this involves monthly investments or investments from distributions, it can help if you map out how all investments will be made at the beginning of the year so you don't have to think too much at the point at which the payment is received. That could coincide with a hearing or other important work task, making it difficult to focus on your personal finances at this time. The more you can automate investments within a period, the more likely it is they will happen as planned and therefore the closer you will get to your long-term goals.

Review/forward planning

There comes a time to take stock and review. When I do these meetings with our clients, I call them forward planning meetings, as while we are looking at what has happened previously, our real focus is what will happen in the future. I would recommend this happens annually. While you can do it more often, my intention is to build a relatively low-maintenance approach rather than something that requires your constant attention.

This process should take place when you have sufficient time and mental capacity. While it doesn't need to take long, you do need to be able to think clearly and without feeling under pressure, because this process is about reviewing your progress and critically evaluating the plan you have previously prepared.

Let's look at the different stages of the REAP forward planning process:

1. **R**eview
2. **E**xpectations
3. **A**nalysis
4. **P**lan

1. Review

With this first element of forward planning, you will need to pull together information on investment performance and consider whether you have followed the plan you prepared last year:

- Have you made the investments you expected to?
- Was the timing as planned?
- Did you make use of tax breaks efficiently?

This element is about gathering the data you require rather than trying to draw conclusions. It might involve looking back at the previous plan as well as digging out a portfolio value from last year. It can also be helpful to find a suitable benchmark against which to compare investment performance. In this area it is important to compare like for like, so if your comparison is the FTSE 100, for example, and you have selected an investment approach in which half of your portfolio is invested in shares and half in bonds, then a benchmark that is 100% shares is unlikely to be representative. Instead, you could use an IA (Investment Association) Mixed Investment sector with a similar equity content. The IA sectors include all UK investment funds with a similar equity content, so when you compare performance against the sector average, you can see how your fund has performed.

2. Expectations

At this point you are seeking to understand how the reality of the past twelve months has compared with your expectations:

- Over the past year, did things pan out as you expected?
- Is your role still going as you would like?
- Has your income been in line with your expectations?

Sometimes the reality will be in alignment with your expectations, and for some people this alignment persists for many years, but almost inevitably there will be times when the two aspects differ. The impact could be either positive or negative, and the purpose at this stage is to understand any differences and be aware of the impact that they have had, without passing judgement or worrying too much about the differences.

3. Analysis

Now is the time to start to analyse the information you compiled in stages one and two:

- Looking at investments initially, how has your portfolio compared to the appropriate benchmark?

- Is it broadly in line, slightly better, slightly worse, or significantly better or worse?

If the answer to those questions is at one extreme, first check that the benchmark is representative and then try to understand why there has been a discrepancy. For example, in a rising market, if you have taken more investment risk than the benchmark, you would expect that to result in higher growth. In a falling market, the opposite should be true, as more investment risk is likely to see larger falls. It may be that you are entirely comfortable with slightly more risk than the benchmark and are happy to accept that, but if this is not the case, you may choose to change the portfolio slightly.

If you are using a managed investment solution and the portfolio has underperformed your benchmark, I would suggest that, in addition to trying to find the context of underperformance, you look at the performance of the strategy over the longer term. If it has performed above the benchmark in three of the last five years, then unless there is a specific reason to think that the last year's performance is anything other than a one-off, it is probably worth giving it the benefit of the doubt and continuing for a further year. All investment funds and strategies, if taking active calls on either asset mix or companies, will not get every decision correct, so even the most successful will underperform at times. What you don't want to do is swap and change all of the time and risk selling a great investment on the back of one slightly bad year. By the same token, keeping an investment indefinitely when it is consistently underperforming your benchmark also doesn't make sense.

When reviewing the contributions and investments you have made, consider the differences to your original plan:

- If you did not stick to the plan entirely, why was that?
- Are there reasons you need to tweak the plan to better suit your situation?
- Was there something that happened this year that was beyond the norm, and everything will be back on track next year?
- Did you spend more than you expected on other things and divert money away from investments?

When assessing this element, it is important to be honest with yourself and, if you haven't followed the plan, to understand why. It could be due to circumstances beyond your control (eg distributions were lower than expected), it could be a one-off (eg I needed a knee operation, which cost a significant sum), or it could be an indication that your spending and saving strategy is not right for you. If the latter is the case, you may need to adjust your plan and rework your expectations. It is important to strike the correct balance between living now and saving for the future, though, so if you need to adjust your plan, it might be necessary to compromise on either your future lifestyle or the date that you stop work.

It could be, of course, that you need to have a stern word with yourself and remember what you are working towards, and why it is more important than the things you spent your resources on last year. If you saved more than planned, well done; give yourself a pat on the back. Was this at the expense of your current lifestyle, though? If so, should you do more with your family next year, as you are ahead of target?

4. Plan

With all of the information you have gathered and analysed, you are now ready to consider the forward planning:

- Starting with the long-term plan, does this still represent where you want to get to, and are any adjustments needed?
- Once you have reconfirmed your commitment to the long-term plan and made any required adjustment, it is time to measure progress compared to what was expected; are you on track, ahead or behind?

If the difference is down to either positive or negative market performance, put that aside. We know markets are not linear and that progress is based on averaged returns, so it is entirely normal that market returns will be either more or less than expected in each year. Sometimes, however, you may find that your plan is not on track and needs adjustment. Depending on your circumstances, the adjustment can come from increasing investments or extending timescales. For some, neither may be possible, in which case there could be a requirement to make compromises and adjustments to the plan.

If you are working together as a couple, make sure you make time to discuss the shortfall and work through potential solutions together. A solution you have reached together will be much better than something that is forced upon one partner, potentially leading to a source of conflict. In my experience of going through this process with countless couples, I find people both resourceful and creative in finding alternative solutions and adjustments. It is very often the case that, once the revised target has been achieved, I hear comments like, *I am so glad we made that change, as this is better than our original plan*. This reiterates the importance of recognising that compromises and adjustments are a normal part of the process, and that they can actually improve the plan.

This process should help to recalibrate your long-term planning and leave you energised and refreshed with renewed enthusiasm and motivation, all of which you may need over the next twelve months as you approach new hurdles and challenges but move closer to your dreams.

ARE WE NEARLY THERE YET?

Mary and Robert had a dilemma to contend with. For many years they had worked as freelance proofreaders for legal books. The work had been interesting and varied, and it had allowed them to live a good life on the Devon coast. Over the last couple of years, however, Mary's eyesight had started to deteriorate, making it difficult for her to work in artificial light. During the summer this was less of a problem, with long days of sunlight allowing work at the same intensity as before, but in winter Mary was struggling. Although this was less of an issue for Robert, the general pace of the work was starting to catch up with him too, with him certainly feeling those couple of years that he was older than Mary. Although they had always planned to work until Robert was sixty-five, the next five years were looking to be a bit more of a struggle than they had previously anticipated.

When we spoke about these issues, I suggested we look in more depth at the cost of Robert and Mary's lifestyle, and I asked them to work out their day-to-day living expenses. We then also considered the trips they would like to take and other significant expenditure. I compared this with the assets they had already accumulated and their future inflows from pensions and other income sources.

This demonstrated they could afford to retire immediately rather than working for a further five years, as they had planned. While Mary and Robert took some time to consider this outcome and we ran through the numbers on a couple of occasions, just to make sure they were comfortable, initially they took no action. A few months later, however, they decided to go to Australia for three weeks and were able to tell their biggest and most demanding client that they would be away for three weeks, comfortable in the knowledge that if that meant the client sought alternative proofreaders, it wouldn't be catastrophic for Robert and Mary.

This started the process of being choosier about the work they took on. They avoided complex work with tight deadlines, which they had previously felt compelled to accept and which put them under intense pressure and increasing stress levels. They used their additional spare time to walk along the beach every day, instead of only looking at it out of the window while they worked.

Eighteen months from the point at which I told them they could retire, Robert and Mary took the final step to retire fully, comfortable in the knowledge that their finances were secure and they no longer needed to work. Our meetings thereafter were filled with discussions about all of the interesting things they were doing, now that they didn't have to spend time working.

Summary: Forward planning

We have run through a framework for future planning and review – REAP – as follows:

- Review – assess progress at least annually
- Expectations – consider how the progress compared with what you thought would happen
- Analysis – understand differences between expectations and reality, assess investment performance and consider your actions in implementing the plan
- Plan – use all of this information to adjust, amend or reconfirm your financial plan for the coming twelve months

By following the REAP approach annually, you will ensure your plan remains relevant to your current plans and on track to provide the future you desire.

15
Thriving As Partner

While a good number of legal professionals never aspire to become a partner, often due to the high levels of stress involved, many see the role of partner as the ultimate achievement of their career. If you hope one day to become a partner, if you have recently achieved that promotion, or if you have enjoyed the position for a number of years, this chapter gives advice specific to the different financial considerations required.

Now that you are a partner

After many years of hard work, your efforts have finally been recognised, and you have been promoted to partner in your firm. Congratulations – it's a fantastic achievement, and you should feel proud. In many ways, though, the hard work starts now. Before it was about hard graft and putting the hours in; now you need to work smarter. While I can provide no insight into how to make a success of being a partner, I have worked with a number of senior associates as they have navigated this transition from a personal finance perspective.

Until now the firm has provided most of the financial products you need. There is a pension scheme to which the firm contribute, and you will have received life insurance and, most likely, private medical and critical illness cover. You haven't really had to think too much about it. You have been subject to PAYE, meaning that all of the tax relating to your employment has been deducted from your salary (and bonus) before you receive it. Now, in theory, everything is down to you. You also have to navigate partnership capital contributions as well as understanding drawings and distributions.

In reality, many firms include some life insurance as a partnership benefit, with the costs automatically deducted from your distributions, and most will deduct tax from your earnings (and hold that within tax reserves) as well as provide an accountant to prepare your tax returns. However, now that you have so much to do in your day job, let's consider the things you need to understand and the actions you need to take.

Partnership capital

As an owner of the firm, you will be required to contribute some capital to buy your share. The amount will vary depending on the firm, as may the timing of this requirement. There are generally three options for contributing partnership capital, although these are often more restricted for initial partnership capital. Generally, speaking, you can:

- Take out a loan, which the firm will typically have negotiated with a bank
- Provide the capital from your own reserves, if you have them
- Pay from future distributions, though this option will generally not be available to new partners

In most cases the loan will be the best option at this stage. It means you are not tying up your own capital, and as it is a qualifying business loan, the interest is tax-deductible, meaning you do not face the full brunt of the interest payments. When you eventually leave the partnership, your capital contribution will be repaid, and this will be used to pay off the loan, which makes this an interest-only loan secured on your share of the partnership.

Over your time in the partnership, and particularly as you move up the scale of partnership points (or whatever mechanism is used for increasing earnings as you become more senior), there will be further requirements for capital, and each time you can select whether to take the loan or provide from cash or distributions. In the first few years the loan is likely to be the best option for you. It ensures you have access to as much of your distributions as possible for your own planning rather than receiving cash back once you eventually leave the partnership, but you have the opportunity to select from the finance options above for each capital contribution, so you can use different methods to fund partnership capital over time.

There is often also something called *dribble capital,* which is included in the amount deducted from your income to cover your tax liabilities. Typically, a small amount each year will be added to your capital contribution from these funds, meaning that even if you were to use the loan throughout your career without ever making a capital contribution yourself (which many partners do), you would still receive a small amount of capital when you retire from the partnership.

Clearly, in the event of insolvency of the partnership, you will lose some or all of your partnership capital. This will be the case if you have taken out the loan or put the money in yourself, but in the case of a loan, you will be liable for repayment of that loan. While this is a very real and credible risk, and there have been a number of law firms that have failed over the years, if you are part of a larger firm, you may feel this risk is relatively small. It would be prudent, though, to be aware of this risk and ensure that you keep some capital easily accessible in the event of the failure of the firm. Whether that needs to be all of your outstanding loans would depend on the perceived risk, but in all cases I advise you keep at least some cash reserves to cover this eventuality. In the past I have come across partners who keep all assets in their spouses' names to ensure they are protected against insolvency of the partnership, although with the advent in 2001 of limited liability partnerships, this more extreme action is generally not required.

Protection

Any death in service benefits that were provided to you as an associate of the firm will end when you become a partner. Some partnerships include life insurance, critical illness and even income protection. Taking out this life insurance cover is typically optional, and in some cases you can choose the level of cover that is provided.

Some firms make no such provision, and it is down to you to put cover in place. In any case, making your own provision is not the worst idea, as it avoids the threat of cover being cancelled if you leave the partnership, which could happen at a time when it would be expensive or impossible to take out alternative cover due to your age or state of health. If your existing cover will come to an end, you should take a little time to consider any life insurance you will need and take the steps to put something in place. While it is tempting to think you have time and nothing will happen, you need to ensure that your loved ones are protected in the event of your ill health or death. Insurance also gets more expensive as you get older – an extra incentive to deal with this immediately rather than putting it off.

Pension

When you leave employment to become a partner, your membership in the firm's pension scheme will cease, and you will need to make your own provisions. This could be to add to the same pension scheme (which most schemes will allow) or to a new pension scheme of your choosing. It will be up to you to decide how much to contribute, and you will receive no contribution from the firm, as you will no longer be an employee. This will also likely be the point at which you start to be impacted by additional restrictions on the amount you can save into your pension, ie by the tapered annual allowance. The annual allowance is the maximum you are allowed to pay into a pension each year and is currently set at £60,000.

At the time of writing, the tapered annual allowance applies to those with income of more than £260,000 per annum and reduces the annual allowance by £1 for every £2 of income above this level, to a minimum of £10,000. To assist those with temporarily high incomes who have not made significant pension provisions, it is possible to carry forward unused relief from the previous three years. This means that if you didn't use your full annual allowance over the past three years (and most people don't use it all), you can make up some of the allowance that wasn't used.

If your partnership income is likely to be significant (currently £360,000 plus as a first-year partner), you should consider maximising your pension contributions at this stage if you are able to. This will allow you to benefit from 45% tax relief on a significant contribution to your pension. It will also allow you to make real progress towards your long-term savings and ensure that you can build a decent pension provision. This is because, after this initial three years in which you can fill up lower contributions from previous years, you will be restricted to saving no more than £10,000 per annum into your pension (assuming your UK income is more than £360,000 per annum). You must use all of the current year's allowance first, and you can then go back three tax years and fill in that allowance, repeating the exercise for the next two tax years.

Here's an example of pension contributions for a new partner:

Income: £500,000

Previous pension contributions:

1. £25,000
2. £20,000
3. £18,000

Annual allowance for current tax year is tapered to £10,000, but looking back, the contribution over three years ago was £18,000. For an associate the annual allowance was unlikely to be tapered; therefore, £42,000 of unused relief is available (£60,000 – £18,000).

Note: Annual allowance increased from £40,000 to £60,000 in the 2023/24 tax year, so if three years ago is before then, you should use £40,000 as opposed to £60,000 within the calculation.

The minimum contribution you should make this year to ensure you use the pension allowance that would otherwise be lost is £52,000 (this year's allowance plus £42,000 unused allowance from three years ago). This will require you to make a payment of £41,600, as 20% tax relief is provided at source. You will then receive additional tax relief of 25% (in this example £13,000) through a reduction in your tax bill at the end of the tax year, resulting in a net cost to you of £28,600 (£41,600 – £13,000) and adding £52,000 to your pension.

The following year you would do the same calculation for what is now your pension contribution from three years ago. In this case the contribution was £20,000, so the unused relief is £40,000. Again, you must first use this year's allowance, but due to your earnings this will be restricted to £10,000. Your total contribution would therefore be £50,000, requiring you to make the contribution of £40,000 (as 20% tax relief is provided immediately) with additional tax relief of £12,500 being provided through your tax return. This reduces your overall net cost to £27,500 for a £50,000 pension contribution.

In the third year the figures would be £35,000 of unused relief and the same £10,000 current year contribution, with a total of £45,000, requiring a payment of £36,000 (again 20% relief would be provided straight away). Additional tax relief through your tax return will be £11,250, giving an overall net cost of £24,750 for your £45,000 pension contribution.

Thereafter, you will be able to contribute only £10,000 gross per annum due to your income resulting in a tapered annual allowance, and as you will have used your full allowance in each of the last three years, there is no unused relief available. This will cost you £5,500 in total once all reliefs have been provided.

Using this method, you will have been able to boost your pension fund by £147,000 over three years, at a cost to you of £80,850. While this may be a period in which you feel you have other financial priorities, there is a huge benefit to have made these pension contributions, as you are unlikely to have another opportunity to boost your pension in this way again while you remain a partner in your firm. The money you have put into your pension should then have a long time to grow tax-free and will provide a good basis for your long-term financial planning.

Buy the big house

Naturally, once you reach your goal of becoming a partner, thoughts turn to the things that will make a real difference to your lifestyle. The biggest of these is your home, and you will be able to afford a bigger, more expensive property than was the case as an associate. If, like most of the people I work with, you are a partner in London, you are faced with the prospect of a significant cost to buy a new house and the decision on how far a commute you are willing to accept. Remember that, with your increased workload as a partner, you really don't want a long commute.

My suggestion here would be to hold fire for a couple of years, if you are able to. I suggest this for three main reasons:

- **Income.** It will take a year or so before your partnership income really starts to flow, so for the first six months you may find your actual take-home income has not really changed much at all. It is only when you have accumulated two or three distributions that you will start to feel you are making any progress at all on your finances.

- **Pension.** It is sensible to make the pension contributions outlined earlier. While this may, understandably, not feel like a priority now, your older self will thank you for your foresight!
- **Costs and convenience.** Because of the impact of stamp duty on the purchase of high-end houses, it makes sense to keep the number of moves to a minimum. This means either buying your 'forever home' next or making no more than two further moves. The problem here is the cost of houses in the UK, particularly in easy commuting distance of the office. While lenders will look at multiples of earnings (in which a few years as a partner already helps), in my experience of working with many partners as they have embarked on this journey, when the outstanding mortgage is seven figures, it doesn't feel comfortable, no matter how much you are earning. We also often see scenarios in which the monthly repayments exceed monthly drawings, which again is not a comfortable position.

In my experience, if distributions are strong, that mortgage can be reduced to a manageable level fairly quickly, so I mention these challenges not to say that you shouldn't take this step. Most do, and you probably will yourself, and that is actually pretty good long-term planning. My suggestion would simply be to hold off for a couple of years, build up some capital and enjoy having those distributions without significant additional commitments for them for a while, before taking the plunge and buying the big house.

Once you have bought the house, investing while paying off the mortgage does make good sense from a financial perspective. However, from a psychological standpoint for most partners I have worked with, a better approach is focusing on paying down the mortgage in the early years and therefore reducing the financial stress you may feel. I normally suggest partners make use of ISA and pension allowances during this period (as they can be lost if not used) but get the mortgage down to a level that doesn't frighten them every time they get a mortgage statement!

Once your monthly mortgage payments are down to a level at which, together with your living expenses, you are able to live within your drawings for day-to-day expenses, you will feel comfortable directing more of your surplus distributions towards investment rather than focusing solely on debt reduction.

Put a little time into your own financial planning

The demands on a partner of a law firm are significant, and this can take up all of your intellectual energy, particularly in your early days as a partner and when dealing with complex cases. It is important, however, to set aside some time for financial planning. Whether this involves you doing the planning work yourself or working with an adviser, you should allocate at least a couple of hours every six months for this purpose. This would normally be towards the end of February for anything which is critical to tax year end. The other time for review may coincide with a quieter period in your area of practice or just before distributions are due. You can then plan investments around when distributions will arrive, which will help to avoid the anxiety of having too much money in your current account, which can happen without adequate planning. If this forward planning work is done efficiently, your February review, which is there to catch missing deadlines for things like ISAs and pensions, when allowances could be lost if not used, may be quite brief.

If you choose to self-manage, you need to be disciplined about setting aside the time for planning, which can be difficult in busy periods. When you consider your investment strategy, you also need to be mindful of the amount of time you can dedicate to your own finances. While you may enjoy selecting investments and trading shares in companies, you have to consider whether you are consistently going to be able to allow the time required for this when your workload is significant. If you are no longer going to be able to allocate the required time to this, you may be better served with a strategy that doesn't require as much regular input from you.

As partners become more senior and often busier, I tend to find that many want to delegate some of this work to a professional. The advantage of this approach is that your adviser will generally contact you regularly to make sure you put the time aside to do the financial planning work as well. They will of course also have the expertise of going through this process with many people with similar circumstances and requirements, rather than you having to work it all out for yourself. There are naturally costs involved with seeking professional help, which will reduce the returns you receive, although research indicates that individuals with financial advisers tend to achieve better outcomes than those who seek to self-manage. A part of this is based around investment psychology and ensuring that the emotional aspect of investment is managed, to avoid making suboptimal investment decisions that are driven by fear or greed.

If you select to work with a planner, I recommend selecting a chartered or certified financial planner, as these are the most qualified advisers in the UK. I would also suggest finding somebody who is independent rather than linked to a specific provider or investment solution. In my view, somebody who is more interested in what you want to achieve rather than just your money would be beneficial, and a planning-based rather than product-led approach is generally more likely to help you to get to where you would like to. Most important, however, is finding somebody you feel happy working with. This should be a relationship that lasts for many years, so make sure it is somebody whose company you enjoy!

Summary: Thriving as a partner

Now that you have made partner, we have considered the steps to take from a personal finance perspective. We covered:

- Partnership capital – how it works and what your options are
- Protection – how to put in place the insurance you need so that your planning will not be derailed entirely in the event of ill health or death
- Pensions – why maximising your pension while you have the opportunity makes sense
- Moving – when to upsize your home and some of the things to consider when you do so
- Focus – putting aside some time to plan your financial future, even when work is all-consuming

Taking these steps will ensure that you can really benefit from your hard work as a partner to secure financial freedom and the lifestyle you desire.

Summing Up

We have now gone through the entire DREAM process of financial planning, which will give you the best opportunity to achieve the things that are important to you and your family during the time you have available.

Dream

Let's look once more at the overview of the process and of what is covered at each stage.

Define your vision

We started by considering what you want to achieve over the short, medium and long term. Hopefully, as you went through this process, you managed to gain a realistic impression of how your new future could look and feel. If you do detailed work in this area, you will reap the benefits later. The more real and exciting you can build the picture for the future, and the more joint buy-in you have if planning with your partner, the more likely it is that you will get through the tough times and past the points at which you are tempted to spend your money on things that don't take you towards your long-term aims.

Review your current situation

In Part Two we looked at your current reality. At this stage we took stock of the assets that you have accumulated until now and whether they remain appropriate and helpful towards your long-term goals. We looked at the different types of financial products and cut through the jargon to explain what they are and how they work. We went on to consider your values, why they are important, and how they impact both your financial planning and your investment options and choices.

Establish your plan

Part Three focused on developing your financial plan. We looked at budgeting, why that is important and how to go about it without causing disruption to your lifestyle, while also ensuring that you continue to live today as well as saving for tomorrow. We looked at insurance and making sure your family are protected and can continue to thrive should you suffer from ill health or die. We considered investments in more detail, including different asset classes and how they interact with each other, as well as different investment approaches and whether you should seek professional assistance. With all of this information you were able to build your financial plan, including determining your level of savings and how they will be allocated to allow you to achieve your financial freedom and maintain your lifestyle throughout your lifetime.

Act on it

Once the financial plan was built, we started to look at how we can bring it to life. This requires the establishment of holdings or adding to your existing assets. We discussed how much you will need to accumulate to achieve your objectives and how to deal with secured income such as state pension, which might arrive at a later date than you would like. We considered what would be a great outcome for you and how that can differ between individuals. We then looked at the setbacks you may experience and how to ensure that you follow through on your planning and avoid unnecessary anxiety about the future. These steps can be important to ensure that the financial plan you have spent time developing is actually implemented rather than being a nice idea that falls by the wayside.

Monitor and modify

With the financial plan up and running, we covered the REAP review process, which provides a framework to ensure that your plan remains on track and working as intended. As you are planning over a very long term, it is almost inevitable that there will be changes in relation to what you are able to save, what you want to achieve or, in most cases, both. For some these changes are simply an evolution of their thinking and a development of ideas; for others the changes are fundamental and require the entire plan to be rewritten. Whatever the change is for you, it is a natural part of progress towards your goals. Life will throw things at you that you don't or can't anticipate, so your planning needs to be flexible enough to allow you to adjust, define and amend your financial plan over time.

By following the DREAM process, you will build a future life by design rather than by default. While the default option can lead to a good outcome, that is often not the case. I have come across many couples who have benefited from significant resources during their working life but have had to accept a much more modest lifestyle in retirement, which most find it hard to adjust to. I have also seen situations where people have worked harder and for longer than they needed to secure a fulfilling future for themselves, sometimes to the detriment of their health or relationships.

By working through the different stages in this book, you can take control of your own destiny and quickly evaluate your options as challenges and difficult decisions are required, preventing you from feeling helpless or forced into situations that are not aligned to your values.

This book cannot guarantee you success in your career in the legal profession – that is down to you. It can, though, ensure that your hard work leads on to an exciting future after law.

Acknowledgements

Writing a book is a project I have been talking about for many years, so to finally finish it has been both rewarding and challenging. I hope you have enjoyed reading it and, more importantly, that it will be helpful to you as you plan your financial future.

I would not have been able to complete this task without significant assistance, and I would like to thank some of these individuals. Firstly, my family have provided me with huge support and encouragement, and I have received practical help with editing from my wonderful wife Jude. My children Anabel and Milo have also been incredibly supportive; I hope they are as proud of this achievement as I am of them.

A number of individuals have helped me to polish the initial rough manuscript. Mathew Agbame, a talented and thorough financial planner. Paul Sylvester-Evans, whose wise words and warm encouragement are greatly appreciated. James Harrison, who provided detailed and constructive feedback. John Nicholls and Sylvia Elworthy, who added a valuable contribution from a lived experience as hugely successful legal professionals. I am enormously grateful and indebted for your assistance in making this book far better than it initially was.

Much of my knowledge and experience in working with individuals in the legal profession came through my time working with the father-and-son team of Michael and John Davey at Michael Davey Financial Management. Their knowledge, insight and approach to financial advice gave me the foundation to become the financial planner I am today. Their commitment to doing the absolute best for their clients in all situations is an example I try to live by every day.

The team at O'Sullivan Financial Planning, whose commitment to excellence and desire to harness every available tool to achieve it are a source of inspiration, even if I am not quite as committed to new technology as Conor!

I would like to also thank the team at Rethink Press for their assistance in getting this book from my head to the bookshelves.

I am hugely grateful to all the clients I have worked with throughout my career, both within and outside of the legal profession. It has been my absolute pleasure to work with you and know that, whether our time together has been long or short, joyful or challenging, I do and have always cared deeply about your future success.

The Author

Jeremy is a chartered financial planner and a fellow of the Personal Finance Society. He has been a financial planner for nearly twenty years, having before that worked for ten years in various roles within financial services. He has specialised in providing financial planning advice to individuals in the legal profession throughout his time as a financial planner and has worked with judges, barristers and corporate lawyers. Jeremy runs his own financial planning practice Timeous, working alongside O'Sullivan Financial Planning, who provide regulatory, compliance and administrative support to Jeremy in delivering financial planning advice to his clients.

Although Jeremy has spent all of his financial planning career working in the City of London, he lives in rural Bedfordshire with his wife Jude, children Anabel and Milo, a Dalmatian called Archie, and British shorthair cats Biscuit and Batman. Jeremy is a huge sports fan, enjoying football, F1 and Rugby Union among other sports, and is a passionate fan of Sunderland AFC, Williams F1 and Northampton Saints.

www.timeous.co.uk

www.linkedin.com/in/jeremy-pooley-financial-planning